NEW TESTAMENT AND MYTHOLOGY

NEW TESTAMENT AND MYTHOLOGY

and Other Basic Writings

RUDOLF BULTMANN

Selected, edited, and translated by
Schubert M. Ogden

FORTRESS PRESS   PHILADELPHIA

Library of Congress Cataloging in Publication Data

Bultmann, Rudolf Karl, 1884–1976.
　The New Testament and mythology and other basic writings.

　Includes index.
　Contents: New Testament and mythology—Theology as science—The problem of hermeneutics—[etc.]
　1. Bible. N.T.—Criticism, interpretation, etc.— Addresses, essays, lectures. 2. Demythologization— Addresses, essays, lectures. I. Ogden, Schubert Miles, 1928–　. II. Title.
BS2395.B83　1984　　225.6′8　　84–47912
ISBN 0–8006–0727–9

K955F84　Printed in the United States of America　1–727

CONTENTS

Preface   vii

New Testament and Mythology (1941)   1

Theology as Science (1941)   45

The Problem of Hermeneutics (1950)   69

On the Problem of Demythologizing (1952)   95

Science and Existence (1955)   131

Is Exegesis Without Presuppositions Possible? (1957)   145

On the Problem of Demythologizing (1961)   155

Index   165

PREFACE

In venturing to call the essays selected for this volume "basic writings" of Rudolf Bultmann, I cannot but recall his reaction to another editor's claim about his work. With evident feeling, he assured Karl Barth that he was not responsible for the title given to his comprehensive reply to his critics of 1952 (in this volume pp. 95–130) in issuing it as "Bultmann's definitive position."* I should like to think, of course, that he would be much more inclined to approve of the title that I have chosen for this translation. But the fact remains that he was not responsible for it either, and that mine is the task of justifying its choice.

In the case of the title essay, this is not hard to do. Aside from the fact that it is perhaps the single most discussed and controversial theological writing of the century, no one knowledgeable of Bultmann's work could doubt its basic importance for his entire contribution. Although the position for which it 'argues was hardly new, having already taken shape in several of his theological essays written during the 1920s, it is nevertheless the classic formulation of this position and as such incomparable in the Bultmannian corpus. This implies, naturally, that Bultmann was, above all, a Christian theologian who did all of his work even as historian and exegete in the service of the church and its witness of faith. But, again, anyone acquainted with the man and his work knows it all to have been done out of just such a self-understanding and, therefore, to have had its basis in the kind of systematic theology for which "New Testament and Mythology" uniquely formulates the program.

*B. Jaspert, ed., *Karl Barth-Rudolf Bultmann Briefwechsel 1922–1966* (1971), 169.

Because this is so, however, the other essays in the volume may also be reckoned among Bultmann's basic writings. In one way or another, and at one level or another, they all have to do with further explaining and defending the same systematic theological position classically formulated in the programmatic essay.

This is no doubt most obvious in the case of the comprehensive reply to his critics already referred to, which is here translated in its entirety for the first time. Next to "New Testament and Mythology" itself, none of his writings is more important for clarifying what he does and does not mean by "myth" and "demythologizing" or for establishing existentialist interpretation as the appropriate hermeneutical principle for Christian theology. It is significant, however, that at the very beginning of this reply he himself refers to the essay, "The Problem of Hermeneutics," as yet an earlier attempt to advance the discussion. By directly addressing the most fundamental problem that his demand for demythologizing raises, at once surveying the modern history of the problem and proposing a constructive solution to it, this writing also shares fully in the basic importance of the programmatic essay. And the same is true of the other 1941 essay, "Theology as Science," which has never been published before even in German, except in the privately circulated protocol of the meeting of "Old Marburgers" in 1979. Here, as in none of Bultmann's previously published writings, he reflects on the nature of theology itself as in its own way properly a science, thereby clarifying the methodological foundations of his whole theological approach.

As for the other three later and shorter essays, they, too, have to do, respectively, with the same basic issues of the meaning of demythologizing and existentialist interpretation, the presuppositions of exegesis, and the nature of theology as a unique historical science. But they also seem to me to be basic in yet another sense of the word, a sense that I have had very much in mind in selecting them. Largely because of my experience in teaching Bultmann's theology, I am convinced that these essays, when taken together, afford direct access to the essential structure and contents of his thought even to the reader unacquainted with his work, if not, indeed, with theology in general. In fact, I strongly recommend even to more experienced readers that they consider reading these last three essays first, in reverse order, before going on to "New Testament and Mythology" and the other longer and more technical writings.

Either way, careful reading of these seven writings can be counted on to yield a basic understanding of Bultmann's thought as a Christian theologian. And this is the claim, albeit the only claim, that I understand myself to be making in issuing them together as his basic writings. Now as before, scholars seeking to understand the full scope and details of Bultmann's work, particularly his historical and exegetical work, have no alternative but to read all of the writings that document it. But, unless I am mistaken, here at last is a single volume from which even beginning students can understand the basic point of his work. This at any rate is the goal I have had since the inception of this project, and I view it as a fitting way of marking the one-hundredth anniversary of his birth.

So far as the translation is concerned, I have sought above all else to carry over into English Bultmann's scrupulous attention to the verbal formulation of his thought. As is abundantly clear from these essays, he understood the distinctive task of theology to lie precisely in securing the appropriate concepts in which to interpret the Christian witness. But readers of most of the English translations of his writings could be pardoned for failing to appreciate how diligently he himself labored at this task and how careful he was about his own theological conceptuality. Even his *termini technici* have been rendered by such different English expressions (in the same translation!) as to be no longer recognizable for what they are. Of course, any translation is an interpretation, and the present one is certainly no exception. I have been particularly aware of this in my attempt to render his thought in a more inclusive language than he, like many of the rest of us, was wont to use. (As happy as it may be for this purpose to substitute English formulations in the plural for Bultmann's German formulations in the masculine singular, it does risk losing his point in contexts where the stress falls importantly on an existentialist understanding of the single individual.) Nevertheless, I am satisfied that his deepest meaning not only allows for, but, in our situation today, even requires the intentionally nonsexist translation that I have tried to provide.

With only a few exceptions, all noted below, I have been able to base my translation on published editions of the German texts as follows: "New Testament and Mythology," on H. W. Bartsch, ed., *Kerygma und Mythos*, 1, 2d ed. (Hamburg: Herbert Reich-Evangelischer Verlag, 1951), 15–48; "The Problem of Hermeneutics," on

Glauben und Verstehen, 2 (Tübingen: J. C. B. Mohr, 1952), 211–35; "On the Problem of Demythologizing (1952)," on H. W. Bartsch, ed., *Kerygma und Mythos,* 2 (Hamburg: Herbert Reich-Evangelischer Verlag, 1952), 179–208; "Science and Existence" and "Is Exegesis Without Presuppositions Possible?" on *Glauben und Verstehen,* 3 (Tübingen: J. C. B. Mohr, 1960), 107–21, 142–50; and "On the Problem of Demythologizing (1961)," on *Glauben und Verstehen,* 4 (Tübingen: J. C. B. Mohr, 1965), 128–37. The remaining essay, "Theology as Science," is based for the most part on *Protokoll der Tagung 'Alter Marburger' 2.–5. Januar 1979 in Hofgeismar,* 1–23, although in this case I have also relied throughout on the typescript that provides the basis for the published version of the text.

It remains to express my thanks to all those without whose help this project could not have been completed. I am particularly indebted to Antje Bultmann Lemke not only for permission to include the last-named essay but also for her gift of copies both of the protocol in which this essay is included and of the typescript on which the published text is based. Beyond this she has been kind enough to make available to me a complete typescript of Bultmann's as yet unpublished lectures on "theological encyclopedia," study of which has been formative of the preunderstanding out of which I have translated not only this essay but all the others as well. I am also grateful to Georg Siebeck, Jr., of J. C. B. Mohr for permission to publish all of the essays translated from the several volumes of *Glauben und Verstehen.* Invaluable help in reading and criticizing all the drafts of the translation was given by my assistant, James A. Richardson, Jr., who has also prepared the index. And once again, my secretary, Betty Manning, has capably processed my manuscript into finished copy. Finally, I am grateful to Norman Hjelm of Fortress Press, who was quick to share my vision of the project, and who has been in every way supportive in carrying it out.

S. M. O.

Dallas, Texas
February 1984

NEW TESTAMENT AND MYTHOLOGY:
THE PROBLEM OF
DEMYTHOLOGIZING THE
NEW TESTAMENT PROCLAMATION

(1941)

I. DEMYTHOLOGIZING
THE NEW TESTAMENT PROCLAMATION AS TASK

The Problem

Mythical World Picture and
Mythical Salvation Occurrence
in the New Testament

The world picture of the New Testament is a mythical world picture. The world is a three-story structure, with earth in the middle, heaven above it, and hell below it. Heaven is the dwelling place of God and of heavenly figures, the angels; the world below is hell, the place of torment. But even the earth is not simply the scene of natural day-to-day occurrences, of foresight and work that reckon with order and regularity; rather, it, too, is a theater for the working of supernatural powers, God and his angels, Satan and his demons. These supernatural powers intervene in natural occurrences and in the thinking, willing, and acting of human beings; wonders are nothing unusual. Human beings are not their own masters; demons can possess them, and Satan can put bad ideas into their heads. But God, too, can direct their thinking and willing, send them heavenly visions, allow them to hear his commanding or comforting word, give them the supernatural power of his Spirit. History does not run its own steady, lawful course but is moved and guided by supernatural powers. This age stands under the power of Satan, sin, and death (which are precisely "powers"). It is hastening toward its imminent end, which will take place in a cosmic catastrophe. It stands before

1

the "woes" of the last days, the coming of the heavenly judge, the resurrection of the dead, and the final judgment to salvation or damnation.

The presentation of the salvation occurrence, which constitutes the real content of the New Testament proclamation, corresponds to this mythical world picture. The proclamation talks in mythological language: the last days are at hand; "when the time had fully come" God sent his Son. The Son, a preexistent divine being, appears on earth as a man (Gal. 4:4; Phil. 2:6ff.; 2 Cor. 8:9; John 1:14, etc.); his death on the cross, which he suffers as a sinner (2 Cor. 5:21; Rom 8:3), makes atonement for the sins of men (Rom. 3:23–26; 4:25; 8:3; 2 Cor. 5:14, 19; John 1:29; 1 John 2:2, etc.). His resurrection is the beginning of the cosmic catastrophe through which the death brought into the world by Adam is annihilated (1 Cor. 15:21–22; Rom. 5:12ff.); the demonic powers of the world have lost their power (1 Cor. 2:6; Col. 2:15; Rev. 12:7ff., etc.). The risen one has been exalted to heaven at the right hand of God (Acts 1:6ff.; 2:33; Rom. 8:34, etc.); he has been made "Lord" and "King" (Phil. 2:9–11; 1 Cor. 15:25). He will return on the clouds of heaven in order to complete the work of salvation; then will take place the resurrection of the dead and the last judgment (1 Cor. 15:23–24, 50ff., etc.); finally, sin, death, and all suffering will be done away (Rev. 21:4, etc.). And this will all happen at any moment; Paul supposes that he himself will live to experience this event (1 Thess. 4:15ff.; 1 Cor. 15:51–52; see also Mark 9:1).

Anyone who belongs to Christ's community is bound to the Lord by baptism and the Lord's Supper and is certain of being raised to salvation provided he or she does not behave unworthily (Rom. 5:12ff.; 1 Cor. 15:21ff., 44bff.). Believers already have the "first fruits" (ἀπαρχή; Rom. 8:23) or the "guarantee" (ἀρραβών; 2 Cor. 1:22; 5:5), that is, the Spirit, which works in them, bearing witness that they are children of God (Rom. 8:15; Gal. 4:6) and guaranteeing their resurrection (Rom. 8:11).

The Impossibility of Repristinating the Mythical World Picture

All of this is mythological talk, and the individual motifs may be easily traced to the contemporary mythology of Jewish apocalypticism and of the Gnostic myth of redemption. Insofar as it is mythological talk it is incredible to men and women today because for them the mythical world picture is a thing of the past. Therefore, contemporary Christian proclamation is faced with the question whether, when it demands faith from men and women, it expects them to acknowledge this mythical world picture of the past. If this is impossible, it then has to face the question whether the New Testament proclamation has a truth that is independent of the mythical world picture, in which case it would be the task of theology to demythologize the Christian proclamation.

Can Christian proclamation today expect men and women to acknowledge the mythical world picture as true? To do so would be both pointless and impossible. It would be pointless because there is nothing specifically Christian about the mythical world picture, which is simply the world picture of a time now past that was not yet formed by scientific thinking. It would be impossible because no one can appropriate a world picture by sheer resolve, since it is already given with one's particular historical situation. Naturally, it is not unalterable, and even an individual can work to change it. But one can do so only insofar as, on the basis of certain facts that impress one as real, one perceives the impossibility of the prevailing world picture and either modifies it or develops a new one. Thus, the world picture can be changed, for example, as a result of Nicolaus Copernicus's discovery or as a result of atomic theory; or, again, because romanticism discovers that the human subject is richer and more complicated than the world view of the Enlightenment and of idealism allowed for; or, yet again, because there is a new consciousness of the significance of history and nationality.

It is entirely possible that in a past mythical world picture truths may be rediscovered that were lost during a period of enlightenment; and theology has every reason to ask whether this may be possible in the case of the world picture of the New Testament. But it is impossible to repristinate a past world picture by sheer resolve, especially a *mythical* world picture, now that all of our thinking is irrevocably formed by science. A blind acceptance of New Testament mythology would be simply arbitrariness; to make such acceptance a demand of faith would be to reduce faith to a work, as Wilhelm Herrmann made clear, one would have thought, once and for all. Any satisfaction of the demand would be a forced *sacrificium intellectus*, and any of us who would make it would be peculiarly split and untruthful. For we would affirm for our faith or religion a world picture that our life otherwise denied. Criticism of the New Testament is simply a given with modern thinking as it has come to us through our history.

Experience and control of the world have developed to such an extent through science and technology that no one can or does seriously maintain the New Testament world picture. What sense does it make to confess today "he descended into hell" or "he ascended into heaven," if the confessor no longer shares the underlying mythical world picture of a three-story world? Such statements can be confessed honestly only if it is possible to divest their truth of the mythological representations in which it is expressed—provided there is such a truth, which is the very thing theology has to ask. No mature person represents God as a being who exists above in heaven; in fact, for us there no longer is any "heaven" in the old sense of the word. And just as certainly there is no hell, in the sense of a mythical underworld beneath the ground on which we stand. Thus, the stories of Christ's descent and ascent are finished, and so is the expectation of the Son of man's coming on the clouds of heaven and of the faithful's being caught up to meet him in the air (1 Thess. 4:15ff.).

Also finished by knowledge of the forces and laws of nature is faith in spirits and demons. For us the stars are physical bodies whose motion is regulated by cosmic law; they are not demonic beings who can enslave men and women to serve them. If they have any influence on human life, it takes place in accordance with an intelligible order and is not due to their malevolence. Likewise, illnesses and their cures have natural causes and do not depend on the work of demons and on exorcising them.[1] Thus, the wonders of the New Testament are also finished as wonders; anyone who seeks to salvage their historicity by recourse to nervous disorders, hypnotic influences, suggestion, and the like only confirms this. Even occultism pretends to be a science.

We cannot use electric lights and radios and, in the event of illness, avail ourselves of modern medical and clinical means and at the same time believe in the spirit and wonder world of the New Testament.[2] And if we suppose that we can do so ourselves, we must be clear that we can represent this as the attitude of Christian faith only by making the Christian proclamation unintelligible and impossible for our contemporaries.

Mythical eschatology is finished basically by the simple fact that Christ's parousia did not take place immediately as the New Testament expected it to, but that world history continues and—as every competent judge is convinced—will continue. Anyone who is convinced that the familiar world will end in time pictures this end as the result of natural development, as a natural catastrophe, and not as the mythical occurrence that the New Testament talks about; and if one interprets this occurrence in terms of natural scientific theories, like the probationer in the parsonage at Nöddebo, one thereby criticizes the New Testament without knowing it.

What is involved here, however, is not only the criticism that proceeds from the world picture of natural science, but also—and even more so—the criticism that grows out of our self-understanding as modern persons.

Interestingly enough, we moderns have the double possibility of understanding ourselves either completely as nature or as spirit as well as nature, in that we distinguish our true selves from nature. In either case, we understand ourselves as unified beings who ascribe their feeling, thinking, and willing to themselves.[3] We do not understand ourselves to be as peculiarly divided as the New Testament represents us, so that alien powers can intervene in our inner life. We ascribe to ourselves an inner unity of states and actions, and we call any person who imagines this unity to be split by the intervention of divine or demonic powers a schizophrenic.

Even if we understand ourselves as natural beings dependent to the highest degree, as in biology or psychoanalysis, we do not look upon our dependence as being given over to alien powers from which we distinguish ourselves. Rather, we look upon it as our true being, over which we are in turn able to take dominion by understanding, so that we can rationally organize our life. If, on the other hand, we understand ourselves as spirits, we do indeed know that we are always conditioned by our physical bodies, but we distinguish our true selves from them and know ourselves to be independent and responsible for our dominion over nature.

In both cases what the New Testament has to say about the "Spirit"

($\pi\nu\epsilon\hat{\nu}\mu\alpha$) and the sacraments is absolutely alien and unintelligible to us. Those of us who understand ourselves in purely biological terms do not understand how a supernatural something or other like the $\pi\nu\epsilon\hat{\nu}\mu\alpha$ could intervene in the closed context of natural forces and be effective in us. Those of us who are idealists do not understand how a $\pi\nu\epsilon\hat{\nu}\mu\alpha$ that works like a natural force could affect and influence our spiritual attitude. We know ourselves to be responsible for our own existence and do not understand how through water baptism a mysterious something or other could be communicated to us that would then become the subject of our intentions and actions. We do not understand that a meal is supposed to mediate a spiritual power to us and that an unworthy reception of the Lord's Supper is to result in physical illness and death (1 Cor. 11:30), unless, of course, we have recourse to suggestion to explain it. We do not understand how anyone can permit him- or herself to be baptized on behalf of the dead (1 Cor. 15:29).

There is no need to go into details about the special forms that the modern world view assumes in idealism and naturalism. For the only criticism of the New Testament that can be theologically relevant is that which arises necessarily out of our modern situation. A biological world view, for example, is not necessary in the present situation, because its choice is a question of decision within this situation. The only question that is relevant for theology is what can justify the decision for a consistent biological world view, what is the common basis on which the question of decision can arise. But this is, in the first place, the world picture formed by modern natural science and, in the second place, our own self-understanding, according to which we each understand our self to be a closed inner unity that is not open to the interference of supernatural powers.

It is also the case that neither naturalists nor idealists can understand death as the punishment for sin; for them, death is a simple and necessary natural process. If it is no problem at all for naturalists, it is a problem for idealists precisely because it is a natural process. For, being natural, it does not grow out of my true, spiritual self but rather destroys my self. The problem is that human beings are spiritual selves who are different from plants and animals, and yet they, too, are caught in nature, in that they are born, grow up, and die like any animal. But we cannot understand this fact to be a punishment for our sin; for even prior to our having become guilty we were already subject to death. Nor can we understand that in consequence of the guilt of our ancestors we should be condemned to the death of a natural being, because we know of guilt only as a responsible act and therefore regard original sin, in the sense of a quasi-natural hereditary illness, as a submoral and impossible concept.

Just for this reason we also cannot understand the doctrine of substitutionary atonement through the death of Christ. How can my guilt be atoned for by the death of someone guiltless (assuming one may even speak of such)? What primitive concepts of guilt and righteousness lie behind any such notion? And what primitive concepts of God? If what is said about Christ's atoning death is to be understood in terms of the idea of sacrifice, what kind of primitive mythology is it according to which a divine being who has become man atones with his blood for the sins of humanity? Or if it is to be understood in legal terms, so that in the transactions between God and human beings God's demands are satisfied by the death of Christ, then sin can only be understood juristically as outward transgression of a divine command, and ethical standards are simply excluded. Moreover, if the Christ who suffered death was God's Son, a preexistent divine being, what could it mean to him to assume death? Clearly, death does not mean very much to someone who knows that after three days he will rise again!

Likewise, we moderns cannot understand Jesus' resurrection as an event whereby a power to live is released that we can now appropriate through the sacraments. For those who think biologically such talk is utterly pointless, because the problem of death does not even arise. And while for idealists it is meaningful to speak of a life that is not subject to death, the possibility that such a life should be created by a dead person's being brought back to physical life is unimaginable. If God creates life for human beings by any such means, God's action is evidently tied up with natural occurrences in some completely unintelligible way. We can see God's act only in an occurrence that enters into the reality of our own true life, transforming us ourselves. But we cannot understand a miraculous natural event such as the resuscitation of a dead man—quite apart from its being generally incredible—as an act of God that is in this sense of concern to us.

7

As for the Gnostic scheme of ideas, it is only with great effort that we can even put ourselves into a way of thinking according to which the dead and risen Christ was not simply a man, but a God-man, whose dying and rising again were not an isolated fact occurring only to him as an individual person but rather a cosmic occurrence into which we all are drawn (Rom. 5:12ff.; 1 Cor. 15:21ff., 44b). We certainly cannot think this way ourselves because it represents the human self as nature and the salvation occurrence as a natural process. This is also to say that the idea of a preexistent heavenly Christ and the correlative idea of our own translation into a heavenly world of light, in which the self is supposed to receive heavenly garments and a pneumatic body, are not only rationally incredible but also say nothing to us. For we do not understand that our salvation, in which we would find the fulfillment of our life, our authenticity, should consist in such a condition.

The Task

Not Picking and Choosing

Does it follow from such a critical dismantling of New Testament mythology that the proclamation of the New Testament in general is critically set aside?

One thing is certain: it cannot be saved by reducing the amount of mythology through picking and choosing. We cannot, for example, reject the notions of the physical ill-effects of unworthily receiving the Lord's Supper and baptism on behalf of the dead and yet retain the idea that physical food has a pneumatic effect. For one mode of representation underlies all New Testament assertions about baptism and the Lord's Supper; and it is precisely this mode of representation in general, not any one notion in particular, that we can no longer accept.

One can, indeed, point to the fact that within the New Testament not all mythological assertions are equally emphasized or occur with the same regularity in all of the writings. The legends of the virgin birth and of Jesus' ascension are encountered only occasionally; Paul and John know nothing of them. But even if one looks upon them as later accretions, this in no way changes the fact that the salvation occurrence still has a mythical character. And where are the limits of such choosing? We can only completely accept the mythical world picture or completely reject it.

Here theologians and preachers owe it to themselves and to the community as well as to anyone whom they would win for the community to be absolutely clear and honest. No sermon may leave its hearers uncertain about what they do and do not have to hold to be true. Above all, it may not leave them uncertain about what the preacher secretly eliminates, nor may the preacher be uncertain about this. In Karl Barth's book, *Die Auferstehung der Toten*, cosmic eschatology in the sense of a "history of the conclusion" is eliminated in favor of a "history of the end" that is not meant mythologically. Barth can deceive himself about this being a criticism of Paul and of the New Testament only because he eliminates everything mythological from 1 Corinthians by forced interpretation. But this is an impossible procedure.

If the New Testament proclamation is to retain its validity, there is nothing to do but to demythologize it. Of course, we cannot set out on this path on the basis of a postulate that the New Testament proclamation must under all circumstances be made viable in the present. On the contrary, we simply have to ask whether it really is nothing but mythology or whether the very attempt to understand it in terms of its real intention does not lead to the elimination of myth. This way of asking the question, however, is made pressing from two sides: by what we know about the nature of myth in general as well as by the New Testament itself.

The Task of Demythologizing as Posed by the Nature of Myth

The real point of myth is not to give an objective world picture; what is expressed in it, rather, is how we human beings understand ourselves in our world. Thus, myth does not want to be interpreted in cosmological terms but in anthropological terms—or, better, in existentialist terms.[4] Myth talks about the power or the powers that we think we experience as the ground and limit of our world and of our own action and passion. It talks about these powers in such a way, to be sure, as to bring them within the circle of the familiar world, its things and forces, and within the circle of human life, its affections, motives, and possibilities. This is the case, say, when it talks about a world egg or a world tree in order to portray the ground and source of the world in a graphic way or when it talks about the wars of the gods from which the arrangements and circumstances of the familiar world have all arisen. Myth talks about the unworldly as worldly, the gods as human.[5]

What is expressed in myth is the faith that the familiar and disposable world in which we live does not have its ground and aim in itself but that its ground and limit lie beyond all that is familiar and disposable and that this is all constantly threatened and controlled by the uncanny powers that are its ground and limit. In unity with this myth also gives expression to the knowledge that we are not lords of ourselves, that we are not only dependent within the familiar world but that we are especially dependent on the powers that hold sway beyond all that is familiar, and that it is precisely in dependence on them that we can become free from the familiar powers.

Therefore, the motive for criticizing myth, that is, its objectifying representations, is present in myth itself, insofar as its real intention to talk about a transcendent power to which both we and the world are subject is hampered and obscured by the objectifying character of its assertions.

For this reason the mythology of the New Testament, also, is not to be questioned with respect to the content of its objectifying representations but with respect to the understanding of existence that expresses itself in them. What is at issue is the truth of this understanding, and the faith that affirms its truth is not to be bound to the New Testament's world of representations.

The Task of Demythologizing as Posed by the New Testament Itself

The New Testament already invites criticism because some of its representations are mutually disharmonious and, in fact, contradictory. Thus, the views of Christ's death as a sacrifice and as a cosmic occurrence or the interpretations of his person as the Messiah and as the second Adam simply stand alongside one another. But there is actual contradiction between representing the kenosis of the preexistent one (Phil. 2:6ff.) and reporting the wonders through which he shows himself to be the Messiah. Likewise, representing Jesus as born of a virgin contradicts the idea of his preexistence. So, too, does faith in creation contradict the notion of the world rulers (1 Cor. 2:6ff.), or "the god of this age" (2 Cor. 4:4), or "the elemental spirits of the world" (στοιχεῖα τοῦ κόσμου; Gal. 4:3); and the view of the law as given by God contradicts the view that it comes from angels (Gal. 3:19–20).

Criticism is especially called for, however, by a peculiar contradiction that runs throughout the New Testament: on the one hand, human beings are cosmically determined, and, on the other hand, they are summoned to decision; on the one hand, sin is fate, and, on the other hand, it is guilt; alongside of the Pauline indicative there is the imperative, and so on. In short, human beings are understood, on the one hand, as cosmic beings and, on the other hand, as independent persons who can win or lose themselves by their own decisions. Hence the fact that many words in the New Testament directly speak to us today, while yet others are unintelligible and remain closed to us.

Finally, we must add that within the New Testament itself demythologizing has here and there already been carried out. Of this more will be said presently.

Earlier Attempts at Demythologizing

The question, then, is how demythologizing is to be carried out. It is not a new task at which theology today is the first to work. On the contrary, everything that has been said up to this point, or something like it, could have been said thirty or forty years ago; and it is really a *testimonium paupertatis* for our theological situation that it has to be said again today. That this is necessary is clearly due to the fact that the demythologizing undertaken by the critical theology of the nineteenth century was carried out in an inappropriate way—namely, in such a way that with the elimination of the mythology the kerygma itself was also eliminated. And the question is precisely whether this is appropriate. If for the last twenty years we have been called back from criticism to simple acceptance of the New Testament kerygma, theology and the church have run the risk of uncritically repristinating New Testament mythology, thereby making the kerygma unintelligible for the present. The critical work of earlier generations cannot be simply thrown away but must be positively appropriated. If this does not happen, sooner or later—provided church and theology continue to exist at all—the old battles between orthodoxy and

11

liberalism will have to be fought all over again. If we may say sche-matically that during the epoch of critical research the mythology of the New Testament was simply *eliminated,* the task today—also to speak schematically—is to *interpret* New Testament mythology. This does not mean that there may not also be mythologumena that are to be eliminated; it only means that the criterion for any such elimina-tion must not be derived from the modern world view but from the understanding of existence of the New Testament itself.[6]

We may orient ourselves for this task by considering earlier attempts to carry it out. In this connection only a brief word is needed about the attempt throughout the whole history of the church to interpret New Testament mythology allegorically, in such a way that mythical events are spiritualized into processes within the soul. This is naturally the most convenient way of evading the critical question, because one leaves everything as it is for a literal understanding, even while dispensing oneself personally from being bound by it and saving oneself in the domain of the soul.

For the epoch of the older "liberal" theology, it is characteristic that mythological representations are simply eliminated as time condi-tioned and inessential while the great basic religious and moral ideas are explained to be essential. One thus distinguishes between husk and kernel. What, according to Adolf von Harnack, is the kernel of Jesus' preaching of the reign of God and its coming? "First, that this reign is something otherworldly, a gift from above, not a product of natural life; second, that it is a purely religious good—inner unity with the living God; third, that it is the most important, indeed, the decisive, thing that we can experience, that it permeates and domi-nates the whole sphere of our existence, because sin is forgiven and our wretchedness banished." Everything mythical is here eliminated: "The reign of God comes in that it comes to individuals, makes its entry into their souls, and they lay hold of it."[7]

The kerygma is here reduced to certain basic religious and moral ideas, to an idealistic ethic that is religiously motivated. But the truth of the matter is that the kerygma is eliminated as kerygma, that is, as the message of God's decisive act in Christ. The great religious and moral ideas are eternal, timeless truths, which first come to conscious-ness in the course of history and are clarified by concrete historical processes. But knowledge of these truths and acknowledgement of them are not bound to the knowledge or acknowledgement of historical epochs or of the historical persons through whom we first become conscious of them: we can recognize their validity and claim at any time. Thus, reflection on history can have a pedagogical importance but it cannot be decisive.

The New Testament, however, talks about an event through which God has brought about our salvation. It does not proclaim Jesus primarily as the teacher who has indeed said things of decisive importance and whom we therefore continue to revere, but whose person is in principle indifferent to anyone who has understood his teaching. Rather, it proclaims precisely Jesus' person as the decisive event of salvation. It talks about his person mythologically. But can this be a reason for setting the proclamation of his person aside as sheer mythology? That is the question.

For the history-of-religions school, which first recognized the full extent of New Testament mythology, the essential thing in the New Testament is not its religious and moral ideas but rather its religion or piety, in relation to which everything dogmatic, and hence also all objectifying mythological representations are secondary and indifferent. The essential thing is religious life, which has as its high point a mysticism that knows itself to be one with Christ, in whom God has taken symbolic form.

Actually, this view correctly sees something essential, namely, that Christian faith is not a religious idealism, that Christian life is not realized in developing the personality or in shaping human community and somehow changing the world but in turning away from the world and becoming free from it. To be sure, this becoming free from the world is not understood eschatologically as it is in the New Testament but rather in terms of a mystical concept of religion: religion is the human longing for something beyond the world, the discovery of another sphere where only the soul can abide, freed from everything worldly. In religion we are alone with God, filled with the powers of a higher, truer world. And religion is expressed, not practically, in somehow shaping life and the world, but in the impractical action of cult. Just such a religious life is evident in the New Testament, not only as an example but as something catching, arousing, and empowering. Thus, the New Testament is an enduring source of power for one's own religious life, and Christ is the imperishable cultic symbol of the Christian community.[8] The community is here understood purely as a cultic community. And if it is of no mean importance that the community is once again recognized in its religious significance—it could play no role at all in the idealistic interpretation—still the question is whether the meaning of the New Testament ecclesia is fully discovered, for it is an eschatological phenomenon of the history of salvation.

Through such interpretation, also, the New Testament proclamation loses its character as kerygma. Here, too, there is no talk of a decisive act of God in Christ which is proclaimed as the salvation event. The decisive question, therefore, is whether precisely this salvation event, which is presented in the New Testament as a mythical occurrence, or whether the person of Jesus, which is viewed in the New Testament as a mythical person, is nothing but mythology. Can there be a demythologizing interpretation that discloses the truth of the kerygma as kerygma for those who do not think mythologically?

The Demand for an Existentialist Interpretation of the Mythological Conceptuality

The theological work that such interpretation requires can be presented here only in its basic features and by means of a few examples. Nor may any impression be given that such work can be done easily and, once one has the recipe, so to speak, in no time at all. On the contrary, it is a difficult and far-reaching task that requires not the work of one individual but the full time and energy of a theological generation.

The mythology in whose conceptuality the New Testament talks is, in all essentials, that of Jewish apocalypticism and of the Gnostic myth of redemption. Both agree in the basic dualistic view according to which the present world and the men and women living in it are under the dominion of demonic, satanic powers and in need of redemption, a redemption that they themselves cannot provide and that can be given them only through divine intervention. And both talk about just such a redeeming act of God: apocalypticism, by talking about the imminent turn of the age that puts an end to this old age and ushers in the new one through God's sending the Messiah; and Gnosticism, by talking about the redemption brought by the Son of God who is sent from the world of light disguised as a man and who, through his destiny and his doctrine, frees his own and makes a way for them to their heavenly home.

These mythologies, also, do not have their point in their objectifying representations, but have to be interpreted in terms of their understanding of existence, that is, in existentialist terms, after the example of Hans Jonas's interpretation of Gnosticism.[9]

The task, then, is also to interpret the dualistic mythology of the New Testament in existentialist terms. Thus, when the New Testament talks about demonic powers that rule the world and under whose power we human beings have fallen, is there in such talk a view of human existence that offers even to us today, who no longer think mythologically, a possibility for understanding ourselves? Of course, this does not mean that we are thereby offered anything like a scientific anthropology, whose correctness could be disputed and whose general validity could be demonstrated by certain facts. Scientific anthropologies always already presuppose a certain understanding of existence, which is—consciously or unconsciously—a matter of decision. Therefore, the issue is whether the New Testament offers us an understanding of ourselves that constitutes for us a genuine question of decision.

II. DEMYTHOLOGIZING IN ITS BASIC FEATURES
The Christian Understanding of Being
Human Being Outside of Faith

What does the New Testament mean by "the world," "this world" (ὁ κόσμος οὗτος), "this age" (οὗτος ὁ αἰών)? The New Testament can talk about "this world" and its princes, prince, or god just like Gnosticism. But there is an unmistakable difference. Although in the New Testament, as in Gnosticism, human beings are fallen under the world and its powers, the one power that plays no role is matter, our bodies as material and therefore sensual. Nowhere is there the complaint that we, our souls or selves, are imprisoned in material bodies or that sense has power over spirit. Therefore, there is also never any doubt about our responsibility and guilt. God is always taken to be the Creator of the world and therewith of our bodily existence; God is also the Judge before whom we are responsible. Consequently, the role of Satan as the lord of this world has to be peculiarly restricted, or if Satan is indeed its lord or god, "this world" stands in a peculiar dialectical relation to the world as God's creation.

"This world" is the world of transience and of death. It is clearly not this as God's creation, for death has come into the world only as a consequence of Adam's fall (Rom. 5:12). Therefore, transience and death are traced back, not to matter but to sin. It is not, as in Gnosticism, that some tragic destiny has imprisoned the purely heavenly soul in the body; rather, death is the wages of sin (Rom. 6:23; see also 1 Cor. 15:56). To be sure, Paul ascribes an effect to the fall of our ancestor Adam that is similar to that talked about by Gnosticism. But he evidently wants to make individuals responsible once again when he says—disharmoniously with his Adam theory—that death spread to all men "because all men sinned" (Rom. 5:12). Is it only the possibility of death, then, and not its necessity that has come into the world through Adam?

Whatever the answer, equally disharmonious with the Adam theory is the constantly repeated assertion that sin together with death goes back to the "flesh" (Rom. 8:13; Gal. 6:8, etc.). But what is meant by "flesh" ($\sigma\acute{\alpha}\rho\xi$)? It is not what is corporal or sensual but rather the whole sphere of what is visible, available, disposable, and measurable, and as such the sphere of what is transient. This sphere becomes a power over us insofar as we make it the foundation of our lives by living "according to it," that is, by succumbing to the temptation to live out of what is visible and disposable instead of out of what is invisible and nondisposable—regardless of whether we give ourselves to the alluring possibilities of such a life imprudently and with desire or whether we lead our lives reflectively and with calculation on the basis of our own accomplishments, "the works of the law." "Flesh" embraces not only material things but also all of our creating and accomplishing insofar as it is concerned with achieving something demonstrable such as fulfilling the demands of the law (Gal. 3:3); to "flesh" belongs every achieved quality and every advantage that we can have within the sphere of what can be seen and disposed of (Phil. 3:4ff.).

Paul sees that human life is burdened with "care" ($\mu\epsilon\rho\iota\mu\nu\hat{\alpha}\nu$; 1 Cor. 7:32ff.). Everyone cares about something. By nature our care is directed toward securing our life. "We put confidence in the flesh" (Phil. 3:3–4), depending on our possibilities and successes in the sphere of what is visible, and consciousness of our security finds expression in "boasting" (καυχᾶσθαι).

This attitude is incongruous, however, given our actual situation, for we are not really secure at all. It is just so that we lose our "life," our authentic existence, and fall subject to the sphere that we suppose we can dispose of in order to achieve security. Precisely this attitude gives the world that could be God's creation for us the character of "this world," the world that is opposed to God. Precisely this attitude first allows the powers on which we are dependent to arise and, because they have now become powers over us, to be represented as mythical realities.[10]

What is visible and disposable is transient, and consequently whoever lives on the basis of it falls subject to transience and death. Whoever lives out of what can be disposed of is given over to dependence on it. This is already clear from the fact that each of us, by wanting to secure ourselves by means of what is disposable, comes into conflict with everyone else and must secure his or her existence over against theirs. Thus arise, on the one hand, envy, anger, jealousy, and strife and, on the other hand, compacts and conventions, everyday judgments and standards. And it all creates an atmosphere that always already encompasses each of us and guides our judgments, that each of us again and again acknowledges, and that we each help to constitute ever anew. Out of this also grows the slavery of anxiety that oppresses all of us (Rom. 8:15)—the anxiety in which we each seek to hold on to ourselves and what is ours in the secret feeling that everything, including our own life, is slipping away from us.

Human Being in Faith

By contrast, a genuine human life would be one in which we lived out of what is invisible and nondisposable and, therefore, surrendered all self-contrived security. This is life "according to the Spirit" or life "in faith."

Such a life becomes a possibility for us through faith in God's "grace," that is, through trust that precisely what is invisible, unfamiliar, and nondisposable encounters us as love, gives us our future, means life for us and not death.

The grace of God is the grace that forgives sin, that is, it frees us from our past, which holds us in bondage. The attitude in which we seek to secure ourselves and therefore grasp at what can be disposed of, clinging to what is perishing or has always already perished, such an attitude is sin, because it is closure against what is invisible, against the future of God that gives itself to us. They who open themselves to grace receive the forgiveness of sin, that is, become free from the past. And just this is what is meant by "faith": to open ourselves freely to the future. Such faith is simultaneously obedience, because it is our turning away from ourselves, our surrendering all security, our renouncing any attempt to be acceptable, to gain our life, to trust in ourselves, and our resolving to trust solely in God who raises the dead (2 Cor. 1:9) and who calls into existence the things that do not exist (Rom. 4:17). It is radical submission to God, which expects everything from God and nothing from ourselves; and it is the release thereby given from everything in the world that can be disposed of, and hence the attitude of being free from the world, of freedom.

This freedom from the world is, in principle, not asceticism, but rather a distance from the world for which all participation in things worldly takes place in the attitude of "as if not" (ὡς μή; 1 Cor. 7:29–31). Believers are lords over all things (1 Cor. 3:21–23); they have the "authority" (ἐξουσία) of which the Gnostic also boasts. But, as Paul says, "I have authority over everything, but I will not give anything authority over me" (1 Cor. 6:12; see also 10:23–24). Believers can rejoice with those who rejoice and weep with those who weep (Rom. 12:15), but they no longer fall subject to anything in the world (1 Cor. 7:17–24). Everything in the world has receded for them into the indifference of things that have no significance in themselves. "For though I am free from all, I have made myself a slave to all" (1 Cor. 9:19–23). "I know how to be abased, and I know how to abound; in any and all circumstances I have learned the secret of facing plenty and hunger, abundance and want" (Phil. 4:12). The world has been crucified to believers, and they to the world (Gal. 6:14). In fact, the power of their new life comes into its own precisely in their weakness, in suffering and in death (2 Cor. 4:7–11; 12:9–10). Precisely when they become conscious of their own nothingness, when they are nothing in themselves, they can be and have everything from God (2 Cor. 12:9–10; 6:8–10).

Thus to exist, however, means to exist eschatologically, to be "a new creation" (2 Cor. 5:17). Apocalyptic and Gnostic eschatologies are demythologized insofar as the day of salvation has already dawned for believers and the life of the future has already become present. This conclusion is drawn most radically by John, who eliminates apocalyptic eschatology altogether. The judgment of the world is not a cosmic event that is still to happen but is the fact that Jesus has come into the world and issued the call to faith (John 3:19; 9:39; 12:31). Those who believe already have life, they have passed from death to life (5:24–25, etc.). Outwardly, nothing has changed for believers, but their relation to the world has changed: the world can no longer concern them; faith is the victory that overcomes the world (1 John 5:4).

Even as the mythological eschatology of Jewish apocalypticism is overcome, so also is Gnostic eschatology. Believers have not received a new "nature" ($\phi\acute{v}\sigma\iota\varsigma$), or their preexistent "nature" has not now become free, nor do they have any guarantee that their souls will now make their heavenly journey. What they are in faith is not something simply given, a condition, of which they can be so certain that libertinism is the result or which they must guard so anxiously that asceticism is the result. Life in faith is not a condition at all such that it could be described unambiguously in the indicative; rather, the imperative must also be used in addition to the indicative, because the decision of faith is not made once and for all but must be confirmed in each concrete situation by being made anew. It is by being made genuinely anew that it maintains itself. Freedom does not mean being released from the demand under which we stand as human beings, but rather it means the freedom to obey this demand (Rom. 6:11ff.). Faith is not having laid hold of but having been laid hold of, and so it is constantly on the way between the "already" and the "not yet," constantly pressing on toward the goal (Phil. 3:12–14).

In Gnosticism redemption is understood as a cosmic process; participation in it by the redeemed has to be realized in the world, their otherworldly existence as believers thereby becoming something given. This happens in demonstrating their "freedom" ($\grave{\epsilon}\lambda\epsilon\upsilon\theta\epsilon\rho\acute{\iota}a$) or "authority" ($\grave{\epsilon}\xi o\upsilon\sigma\acute{\iota}a$) and in pneumatic phenomena, especially ecstasy. The New Testament in principle knows of no phenomena in which what is otherworldly can become something given in the world. To be sure, Paul knows of ecstasy (2 Cor. 5:13; 12:1ff.), but he struggles against valuing it as proof of possessing the "Spirit." Nowhere in the New Testament is the cultivation of psychical experiences set up as a goal; nowhere does ecstasy appear as the high point of Christian existence for which one ought to strive. It is not psychical phenomena but the attitude of faith that characterizes Christian life.

Of course, Paul shares the popular conviction that the "Spirit" manifests itself in wondrous deeds, and he takes abnormal psychical phenomena to be effects of the Spirit. But in face of the charismatic movement in Corinth he becomes aware of the ambiguity of pneumatic phenomena, and by insisting that the "gifts of the Spirit" are all given "for edification" (1 Cor. 14:26), he breaks out of the view of the Spirit as working like a natural force. He does indeed represent the "Spirit" as a mysterious something or other whose possession guarantees resurrection (Rom. 8:11), and he can indeed speak of the "Spirit" as some kind of supernatural matter (1 Cor. 15:44ff.). But it is clear that in the final analysis he understands the "Spirit" to be the possibility in fact of the new life that is disclosed in faith. The "Spirit" does not work like a natural force nor does it become the possession of believers. It is rather the possibility of life that they must lay hold of by resolve. Hence the paradoxical injunction "If we live by the Spirit, let us also walk by the Spirit" (Gal. 5:25). So, too, "being led by the Spirit" (Rom. 8:14) is not a natural process but is an obeying of the imperative not to live "according to the flesh," for the imperative stands in unity with the indicative. We are not relieved of decision: "But I say, walk by the Spirit, and do not gratify the desires of the flesh" (Gal. 5:16). So it is that the concept of the "Spirit" is demythologized.

In that the fruit of the Spirit is enumerated as "love, joy, peace, patience, kindness, goodness, faithfulness, gentleness, self-control" (Gal. 5:22), it becomes clear that the attitude of faith, of being delivered from the world, also makes us open for our fellow human beings. In that we are freed from anxiety, from frantically clinging to what is available and disposable, we are open for others. Paul characterizes faith as "working through love" (Gal. 5:6), and it is just this attitude that he means by being "a new creation" (compare Gal. 5:6 with 6:15).

The Salvation Occurrence

Christian Understanding
of Being Without Christ?

What has happened in the course of this discussion? The Christian understanding of being has been interpreted nonmythologically, in existentialist terms. But has it really been interpreted in the sense of the New Testament? There is one thing that the interpretation has not taken into account, namely, that, according to the New Testament, "faith" is also faith in Christ. The New Testament not only claims that "faith" as the attitude of new and genuine life is first available after a certain time—faith was "revealed," or has "come" (Gal. 3:23, 25)—for that could be merely a finding of intellectual history; it also claims that faith has first become a possibility after a certain time as the result of an occurrence, the Christ occurrence. Faith as obedient surrender to God and as inner freedom from the world is possible only as faith in Christ.

But now the decisive question is whether this claim is a mythological remainder that must be eliminated or demythologized by critical interpretation. It is the question whether the Christian understanding of being can be realized without Christ.

Earlier, in connection with the interpretations proposed by idealism and by the history-of-religions school, the question was whether they did justice to the New Testament in eliminating the Christ occurrence that it takes to be fundamental. This question also arises in connection with our existentialist interpretation. Does it lie among its consequences to eliminate the Christ occurrence or so to interpret it as to divest it of its scandalous character as an occurrence?

It might appear that what is involved is indeed a mythological remainder that needs to be eliminated. And this question needs to be faced in all seriousness if Christian faith is to be certain of itself. For it can achieve self-confidence only if it consistently thinks through the possibility that it is either impossible or unnecessary.

It might indeed appear that the Christian understanding of being can be realized without Christ, that what we find in the New Testament is simply an understanding of being that is discovered for the first time and more or less clearly expressed. Veiled in the garments of mythology, it is fundamentally our natural self-understanding as it is raised to clarity by philosophy, which not only strips it of its mythology but also works over its formulation in the New Testament, correcting and rendering it more consistent. In that case theology would be the predecessor of philosophy—something that can certainly be understood as a matter of intellectual history—which, having been surpassed by philosophy, is now only its unnecessary and tiresome competitor.

So it might well appear when we take a look at what has been done in modern philosophy. Can we say, then, that what is discovered in the New Testament is what philosophy calls "the historicity of human existence"?

Graf Yorck von Wartenburg writes to Wilhelm Dilthey on 15 December 1892: "Dogmatics was an attempt at an ontology of the higher, historical life. Christian dogmatics had to be this contradictory outcome of an intellectual struggle to live because the Christian religion is a matter of the highest life."[11] Dilthey agrees with him:

> All dogmas must be reduced to their universal value for every human life. They were formulated once under a historically conditioned restriction. If they are freed from this restriction, they are . . . indeed the consciousness of the nature of historicity as such, which is beyond both sense and understanding. . . . Hereafter the primary dogmas that are contained in the symbols of the Son of God, atonement, sacrifice, etc. are untenable in their restriction to the facts of Christian history, although in their universal meaning they refer to the most vital content of all history. But in this meaning these concepts lose their reference to the person of Jesus, which in its rigid exclusiveness transforms everything into a special facticity and expressly excludes all other references.[12]

Yorck gives examples of such an interpretation by referring to Christ's sacrificial death and original sin, which are understandable to him because he knows of the "virtual connection" that exists in history:

> Jesus is not someone totally other but a human being and a historical power. A child benefits from the sacrifice of its mother, which is for its good. There is no history at all without such virtual reckoning and transmission of power [footnote: all history is such a transmission of power, not merely Christianity]—as when rationalism does not know the concept of history. And sinfulness—not sin as an individual act—is

something immemorial to the religious on the basis of their experience. Is it not less "loathsome and disgraceful" [as Dilthey had called the dogma of original sin] when we see, as we can see daily, how illness and misery are passed down? The symbols are drawn from the very depths of nature, because religion—I mean the Christian religion—is supernatural, not unnatural.[13]

In the work done in philosophy since Dilthey this appears to be confirmed. Karl Jaspers could transport Søren Kierkegaard's interpretation of Christian being into the sphere of philosophy. Above all, Martin Heidegger's existentialist analysis of human existence seems to be only a profane philosophical presentation of the New Testament view of who we are: beings existing historically in care for ourselves on the basis of anxiety, ever in the moment of decision between the past and the future, whether we will lose ourselves in the world of what is available and of the "one," or whether we will attain our authenticity by surrendering all securities and being unreservedly free for the future. Is this not how we are also understood in the New Testament? When critics have occasionally objected that I interpret the New Testament with the categories of Heidegger's philosophy of existence, I fear they have missed the real problem. What ought to alarm them is that philosophy all by itself already sees what the New Testament says.

Recently this question of whether the Christian understanding of being is not possible without Christ as a natural, philosophical understanding has been raised anew by Wilhelm Kamlah in *Christentum und Selbstbehauptung*. To be sure, there is an express polemic here against the Christian understanding of being as eschatological that rests on a misunderstanding; because the Pauline "as if not" is not taken into account, the freedom from the world that faith involves is understood undialectically as an unambiguously negative relation to the world. But the understanding of being that Kamlah develops as philosophical turns out to be a secularized Christian understanding. His word for the attitude of genuine historicity is not "faith" but "submission," in the sense of submission to the whole of being or to its source, to God. Such submission, which stands in opposition to all highhandedness, is first able to discover the meaning of being by submitting to it in trust. This submission is described as the "release" in which those who submit free themselves by becoming free from everything to which they might cling. Kamlah himself sees that the structure of this submission is akin to the structure of faith when he says:

> The paradoxical nature of being able to trust has again and again been noticed in theology in connection with the beginning of faith. The question has arisen how the individual can come to faith if faith, being the gift of God's grace, is not to be earned by any kind of highhanded striving, and how, therefore, faith can be demanded if it eludes all human efforts. This question has often been left unanswered because it has been overlooked that this is by no means a special problem of Christianity but a basic structure of our natural being.[14]

Thus, in its real essence Christian faith would be natural submission. "As the true understanding of being, philosophy frees natural submission for its complete truth."[15] Therefore, there is no need for revelation.

Even the love through which faith works can be interpreted philosophically in this way as submission to our intimate neighbors. In fact, at this point philosophy is able to correct the New Testament understanding of love insofar as it holds that Christian love destroys "the course of what is lasting in history" and, by breaking the priority of those who are historically near to us in favor of a love that is directed uniformly to all, does not even notice our true "neighbors."[16] By teaching us to recognize our true neighbors as those with whom we are bound together historically, philosophy alone exposes what is truly natural.[17]

Is it really the case, then, that the human attitude that the New Testament calls "faith" is fundamentally our natural attitude as human beings? Obviously, "natural" in this context does not mean what is always already given and can be taken for granted but rather what is appropriate to our authentic nature. If it must indeed be somehow exposed as such, what is needed to expose it is not revelation but only philosophical reflection. Is "faith" in this sense, then, our natural attitude?

Yes and no. Yes, because faith is not, in fact, some mysterious, supernatural quality but is rather the attitude of genuine humanity. And love, also, is no mysterious, supernatural praxis but is rather our "natural" way of acting. The New Testament to some extent confirms the claim of philosophy that faith and love are our "natural" attitude when it understands believers as "a new creation," that is, as those who have been restored to the authentic human existence that is appropriate to creation. The decisive question, however, is whether human beings as they in fact are, are "natural" in this sense, whether they are quite so free to dispose of their nature.

The question is not whether human nature could have been discovered without the New Testament. Of course, as a matter of fact it has not been discovered without the New Testament; there would not be any modern philosophy without the New Testament, without Martin Luther, without Kierkegaard. But this is simply to note a certain connection in intellectual history, and the understanding of existence of modern philosophy is not justified materially by its historical origin. Conversely, the fact that the New Testament concept of faith can be secularized proves that Christian existence is nothing mysterious or supernatural.

The question, then, is whether our "nature" as human beings can be realized, that is, whether we are already brought to ourselves simply in being shown what our authentic "nature" is (or in reflecting on it ourselves). That we have become lost or gone astray to some degree, or, at least, are constantly in danger of doing so by misunderstanding ourselves, obviously is and always has been presupposed by philosophy as well as theology. Even idealism seeks to open our eyes to what we really are, reminding us that we are spirit and that we ought not to lose ourselves in sensuality. Become what you are! Heidegger's philosophy calls us back to ourselves from our lostness in the "one," and even Kamlah knows that genuine historical existence can be completely covered and buried under and that it is especially buried under today by the aftereffects of the Enlightenment that so dominates our modern thinking; even he knows that submission is not an attitude that can be taken for granted, but that we stand under the commandment to submit and that the release that comes through submission is also always obedience.[18]

But philosophy is convinced that all that is needed to bring about the realization of our "nature" is that it be shown to us. "As the true understanding of being, philosophy frees natural submission for its complete truth," which is to say, obviously, that philosophy frees us for true submission.[19] Philosophy seeks to "expose" what is truly natural in us.[20]

Is this self-confidence on philosophy's part justified? In any case, here is its difference from the New Testament, which claims that we can in no way free ourselves from our factual fallenness in the world but are freed from it only by an act of God. And the proclamation of the New Testament is not a doctrine about our "nature," about our authentic existence as human beings, but rather precisely the proclamation of this liberating act of God, of the salvation occurrence that is realized in Christ.

The New Testament says, then, that without this saving act of God the human situation is desperate, while philosophy by no means does or can look upon it as a desperate situation. How is this difference to be understood?

The New Testament and philosophy agree that we can always be and become only what we already are. For idealism we can lead lives as spirits only because we, in fact, are spirits: Become what you are! Heidegger can call each of us to the resolution of existing as a self in face of death because he makes clear that our situation is one of being thrown into nothing; thus we only have to accept being what we already are. For Kamlah the submission that brings release is a meaningful demand because, in fact, we always already find ourselves submitting insofar as we are members of some historical community in which we share through care and service.

The New Testament also sees that we can only be who we already are. And this is just why Paul commands believers to be holy, because they already are holy (1 Cor. 6:11; see also 5:7); to walk by the Spirit, because they already live by the Spirit (Gal. 5:25); and to do away with sin, because they are already dead to sin (Rom. 6:11ff.). In Johannine terms, it is because believers are not "of the world" (τοῦ κόσμου) that they can overcome it (John 17:16), and it is because they are born of God that they cannot sin (1 John 3:9). Eschatological existence can be realized because "the time had fully come" and God sent his Son "to deliver us from the present evil age" (Gal. 4:4; 1:4).

Thus, the New Testament and philosophy agree that we can lead an authentic life only because we are already standing in it and it is already ours. But the New Testament speaks this way only to believers who have allowed God's liberating act to take place in their existence, not to all human beings as such. It disputes the claim that life already belongs to all men and women, and it holds the human situation in general to be desperate.

Why? Precisely because it knows that we can only be and become what we already are and because human beings as such, before and outside of Christ, are not already in their authentic being—in life— but are rather in death.

At issue is understanding the fallenness of life in which all human beings first find themselves—a fact that is not concealed even from philosophy. But while philosophy views such fallenness as a condition that we are able to avoid once we understand our situation, and hence as a condition that does not extend to our very selves, the New Testament claims to the contrary that we ourselves are utterly and completely fallen.

Does this claim about the fallenness of our very selves contradict the fact, clearly attested by philosophy, that we can know about our fallenness? How could we know about it if we were completely fallen, even in our very selves? In truth, the converse is the case: we can know about our fallenness only if we ourselves are fallen, only if we know that we are not who we authentically should be and want to be. Knowledge of our authenticity belongs to our existence as such; we would not exist as human beings at all—even in our fallenness—if we did not know about it, if we were not concerned with what we authentically are. But our authenticity does not belong to us like some natural property, and we do not dispose of it. Naturally, philosophy does not think we do either, but knows that authenticity must constantly be laid hold of by resolve. But philosophy is of the opinion that knowledge of our authenticity already gives us control over it. Although our authenticity is not something that we constantly realize, it is something that we can realize at any time. You can because you ought! Philosophy thus takes a possibility in principle to be already a possibility in fact. But in the opinion of the New Testament, human beings generally have lost the possibility in fact; indeed, their knowledge of their authenticity is falsified by being tied up with the opinion that they have control over it.

Why have human beings in their fallenness lost the possibility in fact of realizing their authentic life? Because in their fallenness any movement is a movement of fallen human beings. Paul makes this clear by showing that and why the Jews who seek "righteousness" lose the very thing they seek—namely, because they want to be "justified" by their own works, because they want to "boast" in the presence of God. This reveals the very human attitude that governs the fallenness under the "flesh" from which the Jews want to escape: the arbitrariness and highhandedness of human beings who are trying to live out of themselves. If genuine life is a life of submission, it is missed not only by those who live by disposing of what can be disposed of instead of by submitting but also by those who understand even submission to be an aim that they can dispose of and do not see that their authentic life can only be an absolute gift.

In the "boasting" of Jews who are faithful to the law, just as in the boasting of Gnostics who are proud of their wisdom, it becomes clear that the basic human attitude is the highhandedness that tries to bring within our own power even the submission that we know to be our authentic being, and so finally ends in self-contradiction. In idealism this leads to talk about *"deus in nobis"*:

> Accept the deity into your own will,
> And it descends from its throne above the worlds.

With Heidegger the sacrilege is not so apparent because he does not characterize the attitude of resolution as submission; it is clear, however, that accepting one's thrownness by resolving to die is an act of radical highhandedness. With Kamlah the proximity to Christianity is relatively great when he says that the commandment to submit can be fulfilled only because God gives Godself to be understood, because being makes trusting submission possible by disclosing its meaning to us, and because submission perceives the hint of meaningfulness in being itself.[21] But the claim that being is meaningful seems to me to be a desperate claim. Is it not desperate highhandedness when Kamlah says, "It is not possible to doubt that being in general is meaningful"?[22] Does this really settle whether the only appropriate attitude for human beings without Christ is to despair of the possibility of their being?

In any case, this is what the New Testament says. Naturally, it cannot prove its claim anymore than philosophy can prove its claim that being is meaningful. It is a question of decision. The New Testament addresses us on the supposition that we are highhanded through and through and that, while we can therefore very well know that we do not in fact have an authentic life, we are also powerless to lay hold of it because we are fallen through and through in our highhandedness.

This means, in the language of the New Testament, that we are sinners; for this highhandedness is sin, rebellion against God. Highhandedness, or "boasting," is sin, because no human being is to boast in the presence of God; "let anyone who boasts, boast of the Lord" (1 Cor. 1:29, 31; 2 Cor. 10:17). Is this simply an unnecessary mythological interpretation of an ontological statement? Is the character of highhandedness as guilt and thus our responsibility before God something that we can understand simply as human beings? Is the concept of sin a mythological concept or not?

The answer to this question depends on whether or how radically not only a Christian but any human being whatever can understand what Paul says to the Christians at Corinth: "What have you that you did not receive? If then you received it, why do you boast as if it were not a gift?" (1 Cor. 4:7). In any case, this much is clear: highhandedness can be understood as something of which we are guilty only if it can be understood as ingratitude. If the radical highhandedness in which we close ourselves against our authentic possibility of living in submission is to be understood as sin, then, clearly, it must be possible for us to understand our existence in general as a gift. But it is precisely this possibility against which we have closed ourselves in our radical highhandedness; for in it we understand our existence as a task that we must assume and carry out. How much we have closed ourselves against this possibility can also become clear in a pessimism that regards life as a burden laid upon us against our will or in talk about a "right" to life, in the claim to be "happy," and so forth. Thus, in our radical highhandedness we are blind to our sin, and just this betrays our radical fallenness. As a consequence, talk about sin seems to us to be mythological. But this does not mean that it really is so.

Talk about sin no longer seems mythological in the moment in which the love of God encounters us as the power that encompasses and upholds us, that upholds us even in our highhandedness and fallenness, that accepts us for what we are not, and thus frees us from ourselves as we are.

If it is the case that we are utterly and completely fallen in our highhandedness, that we can indeed know that we have our authentic life only in submission, and yet cannot realize such submission because for all of our efforts we remain our highhanded selves, then our authentic life becomes a possibility in fact for us only when we are freed from ourselves. But just this is what the New Testament proclamation says to us; just this is the meaning of the Christ occurrence. It says that where we cannot act God acts and has acted for us.

That this is the meaning of the Christ occurrence is perfectly clear. In Pauline terms it means canceling sin and making "righteous," with the "righteousness" that is given by God and not earned by our own "works." Through Christ God has reconciled the world to himself, not counting their trespasses against them (2 Cor. 5:19); God has made Christ to be sin so that through him we might stand before God as righteous (2 Cor. 5:21). For all who believe this, the past, what they have been hitherto, is finished. They are new persons who come into every now as new. They have freedom.

This makes quite clear that the forgiveness of sin is not meant in the juristic sense merely as remission of punishment, so that for the rest the human situation would remain the same.[23] Rather, what is given through forgiveness is freedom from the sin by which we have hitherto been held captive. And this freedom, in turn, is not understood as a natural quality but as freedom for obedience. Alongside of the indicative there stands the imperative. And insofar as all the demands under which we stand are summed up in the demand of love, those of us who are freed from ourselves by God's forgiveness are freed for submission to others (Rom. 13:8–10; Gal. 5:14).

Thus, eschatological existence has become a possibility for us through the fact that God has acted and made an end of the world as "this world," by making us ourselves new. "If anyone is in Christ, he is a new creation; the old has passed away; behold, the new has come" (2 Cor. 5:17). So it is according to Paul. John says the same thing in his language by saying that knowledge of the "truth" of God revealed in Jesus makes us free (8:32), namely, from slavery to sin (8:34). Through Jesus we are called from death to life (5:25), from the darkness of being blind into the light (9:39). Those who believe are "born anew" (3:3ff.) and receive a new origin; they no longer come from the "world" or belong to it, but in faith have overcome it (1 John 5:4).

The occurrence that takes place in Christ, then, is the revelation of the love of God, which frees us from ourselves for ourselves by freeing us for a life of submission in faith and in love. Faith as freedom from ourselves and openness for the future is possible only as faith in the love of God. But faith in the love of God is itself highhandedness as long as God's love is merely a wish or an idea and has not been revealed. Christian faith is faith in Christ because it is faith in the revealed love of God. Only those who are already loved are able to love; only those to whom trust has been given are able to trust; only those who have experienced submission are themselves able to submit. We are freed to submit to God because God has already submitted to us. "In this is love, not that we loved God, but that he loved us and sent his Son to be the expiation for our sins" (1 John 4:10). "We love, because he first loved us" (1 John 4:19).

The submission of God that grounds our submission is expressed in the Pauline statement that God "did not spare his own Son but gave him up for us all; will he not also give us all things with him?" (Rom. 8:32). Or in the Johannine statement that "God so loved the world that he gave his only Son, that whoever believes in him should not perish but have eternal life" (John 3:16). It is also expressed by saying that Jesus has submitted himself for us, "who gave himself for our sins to free us from the present evil age" (Gal. 1:4). "I have been crucified with Christ; it is no longer I who live, but Christ who lives in me; and the life I now live in the flesh, I live by faith in the Son of God, who loved me and gave himself for me" (Gal. 2:19–20).

This, then, is the decisive point that distinguishes the New Testament from philosophy, Christian faith from "natural" self-understanding: the New Testament talks and Christian faith knows about an act of God that first makes possible our submission, our faith, our love, our authentic life.

The question now is whether a limit is thereby set to demythologizing the New Testament proclamation, whether we here stand before a myth or before an event that has a mythical character. What the New Testament says in mythological language about human existence before faith can be demythologized, just as what it says about the existence of believers can also be demythologized. But the question remains whether the claim that the transition from the first kind of existence to the second, our liberation from ourselves for our authentic life, is conceivable only as an act of God, and that faith can be actual only as faith in the love of God revealed in Christ—whether this claim is a mythological claim.*

The Christ Occurrence

Anyone who claims that all talk about an act of God is mythological talk must indeed say that talk about the act of God in Christ is a myth. But whether this is so is here deferred. Even Kamlah holds "mythical talk" about God's act to be also justified philosophically.[24] The question that concerns us now is whether the event in which the New Testament sees the act of God, the revelation of God's love, namely, the Christ occurrence, is a mythical event.

The Problem of Demythologizing
the Christ Occurrence

There is no question that the New Testament represents the Christ occurrence as a mythical occurrence. The only question is whether it has to be thus represented or whether the New Testament itself provides us with a demythologizing interpretation. It is clear, first of all, that the Christ occurrence is not a myth like the cult myths of the Greek or Hellenistic gods. The Jesus Christ who is God's Son, a preexistent divine being, is at the same time a certain historical person, Jesus of Nazareth; and his destiny as a person is not only a mythical occurrence but at the same time a human destiny that ends with crucifixion. The historical and the mythical here are peculiarly intertwined: the historical Jesus whose father and mother are well known (John 6:42) is at the same time supposed to be the preexistent Son of God, and alongside of the historical event of the cross stands the resurrection, which is not a historical event. Certain contradictions indicate how the combination of the mythical and the historical creates difficulties. Alongside of the claim for preexistence (Paul,

---

*The translation of this sentence is based on an emendation approved by Rudolf Bultmann himself in a letter of 23 July 1956. "I must be grateful," he wrote, "for your letter of the 15th, for it brought to my attention that I have been guilty of an oversight in formulating an important sentence. In the short form [sc. of the sentence as it stands in the published text] I intended to say what you have expressed in the longer form; but my short form is wrong, and I am amazed that neither I myself nor my other readers have previously noticed it. I rejoice all the more, therefore, that you have caught the mistake. The sentence must read as you have written," whereupon follows the emended formulation here translated.

John) stands the legend of the virgin birth (Matthew, Luke). Alongside of the statement "he emptied himself, taking the form of a servant, being born in human likeness" (Phil. 2:7) stand the portrayals in the Gospels, in which Jesus' divine being manifests itself in his performing wonders and being omniscient and intangible, as well as the characterization in Acts 2:22, which speaks of "Jesus of Nazareth, a man attested to you by God with mighty works and wonders and signs which God did through him in your midst." Alongside of representations of the resurrection as exaltation from the cross or from the grave stand the legends of the empty tomb and of the ascension.

Thus, the question becomes pressing whether the point of such mythological talk is not simply to express the significance of the historical figure of Jesus and his story, namely, their significance as saving figure and salvation occurrence. If this were their point, their content as objectifying representations could be given up.

It seems clear enough that the point of statements about preexistence or virgin birth is indeed to express the significance of the person of Jesus for faith. What he is for us is not exhausted by, in fact, does not even appear in what he seems to be for ordinary historical observation. We are not to ask about his historical origin, because his real meaning becomes evident only when this way of asking questions is set aside. We are not to ask for the historical reasons for his story, his cross; the significance of his story lies in what God wants to say to us through it. Thus, his significance as a figure is not to be understood in an innerworldly context; in mythological language he comes from eternity, and his origin is not human or natural.

But I shall not now pursue such individual motifs any further. In the final analysis everything is concentrated in the chief question about cross and resurrection.

The Cross

Is the cross of Christ, insofar as it is the salvation event, to be understood only as a mythical event, or can it be understood as a historical event that is the salvation event insofar as it is seen, not in an objectifiable world-historical context but in its significance?

If we follow the objectifying representations of the New Testament, the cross is indeed understood as a mythical event: the crucified one is the preexistent Son of God who becomes man and who as such is sinless. He is the sacrifice whose blood atones for our sin; he bears the sin of the world vicariously, and by taking upon himself the death that is the punishment for sin, he frees us from it. We can no longer accept this mythological interpretation in which notions of sacrifice are mixed together with a juristic theory of satisfaction. But even within the view of the New Testament it does not at all say what it is supposed to say. The most it can say by way of forgiveness is only that the punishment for the sins we have already committed—and are still to commit in the future—has now been remitted. In fact, however, much more should be said, namely, that through the cross of Christ believers have become free from sin as the power that dominates them and hence are also free from sinning. Thus, for example, in addition to the statement "God forgave us all our trespasses and canceled the bond which stood against us with its legal demands; this he set aside, nailing it to the cross," there is the further statement "He disarmed the principalities and powers and made a public example of them, triumphing over them in him" (Col. 2:13–15).

The historical event of the cross is raised to cosmic dimensions. And precisely because the cross is spoken of as a cosmic event its significance as a historical event is made clear in accordance with the peculiar mode of thinking in which historical events are represented as cosmic events, historical contexts as cosmic contexts. If the cross is the judgment of the "world" through which the rulers of this age are brought to nothing (1 Cor. 2:6ff.), this means that what takes place in the cross is the judgment against us ourselves, as those who have fallen under the powers of the "world."

By allowing Jesus to be crucified God has established the cross for us. Thus, to believe in the cross of Christ does not mean to look to some mythical process that has taken place outside of us and our world or at an objectively visible event that God has somehow reckoned to our credit; rather, to believe in the cross of Christ means to accept the cross as one's own and to allow oneself to be crucified with Christ. As the salvation occurrence the cross is not an isolated event that has happened to Christ as some mythical person but rather in its significance this event has "cosmic" dimensions. And its decisive, history-transforming meaning is expressed by representing it as the eschatological event, that is, it is not an event of the past to which one looks back, but it is the eschatological event in time and beyond time insofar as it is constantly present wherever it is understood in its significance, that is, for faith.

It is present, first of all, in the sacraments: in baptism one is baptized into Christ's death (Rom. 6:3) or is crucified with him (Rom. 6:6); in the Lord's Supper the death of Christ is ever and again proclaimed (1 Cor. 11:26); whoever partakes of the Supper participates in the crucified body and the shed blood (1 Cor. 10:16). But then the cross of Christ is also present in the concrete living of believers: "Those who belong to Christ Jesus have crucified the flesh, with its passions and desires" (Gal. 5:24). And so Paul speaks of the "cross of our Lord Jesus Christ, by which the world has been crucified to me, and I to the world" (Gal. 6:14). So, too, he strives to share Christ's sufferings, "becoming like him in his death" (Phil. 3:10).

Crucifying the "passions and desires" also includes overcoming fear of suffering and flight from it and carrying out one's freedom from the world by accepting suffering. Therefore, voluntary acceptance of suffering, in which death is always already at work in us, effects "carrying in the body the death of Jesus" and "being given up to death for Jesus' sake" (2 Cor. 4:10–11).

Thus, Christ's cross and sufferings are present, and how little they can be limited to the past event of his crucifixion is shown when one of Paul's disciples has Paul say: "Now I rejoice in my sufferings for your sake, and in my flesh I complete what remains of Christ's afflictions for the sake of his body, the church" (Col. 1:24).

As the salvation occurrence, then, the cross of Christ is not a mythical event but a historical occurrence that has its origin in the historical event of the crucifixion of Jesus of Nazareth. In its historical significance this event is the judgment of the world, the liberating judgment of us ourselves as human beings. And insofar as this is what it is, Christ is crucified "for us"—but not in the sense of some theory of satisfaction or sacrifice. It is precisely not to mythological but to historical understanding that the historical event discloses itself as the salvation event, insofar as genuine historical understanding understands a historical event in its significance. Basically, the mythological talk seeks to do nothing other than to express the significance of the historical event. In the significance that belongs to it, the historical event of the cross has created a new historical situation; the proclamation of the cross as the salvation event asks its hearers whether they are willing to appropriate this meaning, whether they are willing to be crucified with Christ.

But is the meaning of the historical event of the cross to be seen in it, to be read off from it, so to speak? Does not the fact that the cross of Christ has this meaning lie precisely in its being the cross of Christ? Would not one first have to be convinced of Christ's significance and believe in Christ before one could believe in the saving meaning of the cross? Would not one have to understand it as the cross of the historical Jesus in order to understand it in its meaning? Would not we then have to have recourse to the historical Jesus?

For the first proclaimers this was the case. They experienced the cross of the one with whom they had been bound in the living present. Out of this personal bond, in which the cross was an event in their own lives, it became a question for them and disclosed its point. For us this personal bond cannot be reproduced, and it is not out of it that the point of the cross can be disclosed to us. As an event of the past it is no longer an event of our own lives, and we know about it as a historical event only through historical reports. But this is not at all the way in which the crucified one is proclaimed in the New Testament, so that the point of the cross would be disclosed by his historical life, which is to be reproduced by historical research. On the contrary, he is proclaimed as the crucified one who is at the same time the risen one. Cross and resurrection belong together as a unity.

The Resurrection

But what about the resurrection of Christ? Is it not an utterly mythical event? In any case, it is not a historical event that is to be understood in its significance. Can talking about Christ's resurrection be anything other than an expression of the significance of the cross? Does it say anything else than that Jesus' death on the cross is not to be seen as a human death but rather as God's liberating judgment of the world, the judgment that as such robs death of its power? Is it not precisely this truth that is expressed by the statement that the crucified one is not dead but risen?

In fact, cross and resurrection are a unity as "cosmic" occurrence, as is expressed, for example, by the statement "who was put to death for our trespasses and raised for our justification" (Rom. 4:25). Thus, it is not as though the cross could be seen in itself as Jesus' death and defeat, upon which, then, the resurrection ensued, nullifying his death. He who suffers death is already the Son of God, and his death itself is already the overcoming of death's power. This finds its strongest expression in John when he presents Jesus' passion as the "hour" of his "glorification," and thus understands his "being lifted up" in a double sense, as his being lifted up on the cross and as his exaltation to glory.

Cross and resurrection are a unity in that together they are the one "cosmic" event through which the world is judged and the possibility of genuine life is created. But then the resurrection cannot be an authenticating miracle which one could securely establish so as to convince a doubter that the cross really does have the cosmic-escha-tological meaning ascribed to it.

Of course, it is not to be denied that the resurrection of Jesus is often viewed in the New Testament as just such an authenticating miracle. Thus, it is said that God has provided proof of Christ's claim by raising him from the dead (Acts 17:31). Or, again, there are the legends of the empty tomb and the Easter stories that report demonstrations of the risen one's corporality (especially Luke 24:39–43). But these are undoubtedly later formulations of which Paul still knows nothing. To be sure, even Paul himself once tries to guarantee the wonder of the resurrection as a historical event by enumerating eyewitnesses (1 Cor. 15:3–8). Karl Barth unintentionally shows how fatal Paul's argument is when he tries to interpret away the real point of Paul's statements. According to Barth, Paul's intention in enumerating the eyewitnesses is not to make the resurrection credible as an objective historical fact but only to say that he proclaims Jesus as the risen one in the same way as the earliest community. Thus, the witnesses are intended to be witnesses for the Pauline gospel, not for the fact of the resurrection. For what kind of a historical fact could it be whose reality is connected with the resurrection of the dead?

What kind, indeed! The resurrection of Jesus cannot be an authenticating miracle on the basis of which a doubter can be secure in believing in Christ. This is so not because as a mythical event—a dead person's returning to life in this world (and this is what is involved, since the risen one is perceived with the physical senses)—it is incredible, or because the resurrection cannot be established as an objective fact by ever so many witnesses, so that it could be unhesitatingly believed in and faith would have a secure guarantee. It is so because the resurrection itself is an object of faith; and one cannot secure one faith (faith in the saving meaning of the cross) by another (faith in the resurrection). But the resurrection of Christ is an object of faith because it says much more than that a dead person has returned to life in this world. It is an object of faith because it is an eschatological event. And it is for this reason that it cannot be an authenticating miracle. A miracle, whether or not it is credible, does not attest the eschatological fact of annihilating death's power in general; especially in the sphere of mythical thinking, it is nothing unheard of.

It is clear, however, that throughout the New Testament the resurrection of Christ is the eschatological fact through which Christ abolished death and brought life and immortality to light (2 Tim. 1:10). This is why Paul has recourse to the conceptuality of the Gnostic myth in order to clarify the meaning of Christ's resurrection: as in Jesus' death all have died (2 Cor. 5:14-15), so also through his resurrection all have been raised, only this cosmic occurrence takes place in phases over the course of time (1 Cor. 15:21-22). But as he can say, "in Christ shall all be made alive," so he can also speak of being raised with Christ, just like being crucified with him, as a present occurrence. The sacrament of baptism brings one into communion with Christ's resurrection even as into communion with his death. We not only *will* walk with him in newness of life and be "united with him" in his resurrection (Rom. 6:4-5), but we also already *are*. "So you must consider yourselves dead to sin and alive to God in Christ Jesus" (Rom. 6:11).

Sharing in Jesus' resurrection, like sharing in his cross, proves itself in concrete living: in struggling freedom from sin (Rom. 6:11ff.), and in putting off the "works of darkness," in which the approaching day that will end the darkness is already anticipated: "Let us conduct ourselves becomingly as in the day" (Rom. 13:12-13). "We do not belong to the night or to darkness. . . . Since we belong to the day, let us be sober . . . " (1 Thess. 5:5-8). As Paul wants to share in Christ's sufferings, so he also wants to know "the power of his resurrection" (Phil. 3:10). Thus, he carries in his body the death of Jesus "so that the life of Jesus may also be manifested in our bodies" (2 Cor. 4:10-11). And to the Corinthians who desire proof that Christ is speaking in him he threatens: "Christ is not weak in dealing with you, but is powerful in you. For he was crucified in weakness, but lives by the power of God. For we are weak in him, but in dealing with you we shall live with him by the power of God" (2 Cor. 13:3–4).

Thus, the resurrection is no mythical event that makes the meaning of the cross credible, but it is also believed even as the meaning of the cross is believed. In fact, faith in the resurrection is nothing other than faith in the cross as the salvation event, as the cross of Christ. Hence, one cannot first believe in Christ and then on that ground believe in his cross. Rather, to believe in Christ means to believe in the cross as Christ's cross. It is not because it is the cross of Christ that it is the salvation event; it is because it is the salvation event that it is the cross of Christ. Otherwise it is the tragic end of a noble man.

But then we are once again thrown back on the question, How is it to be seen from the cross that it is Christ's cross, that it is the eschatological event? How do we come to believe in the cross as the salvation occurrence?

Here there seems to me to be only one answer: because it is proclaimed as such, because it is proclaimed together with the resurrection. Christ the crucified and risen one encounters us in the word of proclamation, and nowhere else. And faith in this word is the true faith of Easter.

It would be a mistake, in other words, if one were here to inquire back behind the proclamation to its historical origin as if this could somehow justify it. This would mean that one was trying to justify faith in God's word by historical investigation. The word of proclamation encounters us as God's word, in relation to which we cannot raise the question of legitimation, but which rather asks us whether we are willing to believe it. It asks us this in such a way, however, that in calling us to believe in the death and resurrection of Christ as the eschatological event, it opens up to us the possibility of understanding ourselves. Faith and unfaith, therefore, are matters not of blind, arbitrary resolve but of understanding affirmation or denial.

Such understanding faith in the word of proclamation is the genuine faith of Easter; it is faith that the word being proclaimed is the legitimated word of God. The event of Easter, insofar as it can be referred to as a historical event alongside of the cross, is nothing other than the emergence of faith in the risen one in which the proclamation has its origin. The event of Easter as the resurrection of Christ is not a historical event; the only thing that can be comprehended as a historical event is the Easter faith of the first disciples. The historian can make the emergence of their faith intelligible to some degree by reflecting on their erstwhile personal bond with Jesus; for the historian the event of Easter is reduced to the disciples' visionary experiences. Christian faith, however, is not interested in the historical question; for it—as for the first disciples—the historical event of the emergence of the faith of Easter means the self-manifestation of the risen one, the act of God in which the salvation occurrence of the cross is completed.[25]

The Easter faith of the first disciples, then, is not a fact on the ground of which we believe insofar as it could relieve us of the risk of such faith but itself belongs to the eschatological occurrence that is the object of faith.

In other words, the word of proclamation that arises in the event of Easter itself belongs to the eschatological salvation occurrence. With the judging and liberating death of Christ, God has also established the "ministry of reconciliation" or the "word of reconciliation" (2 Cor. 5:18–19). It is this word that is "added" to the cross and makes it understandable as the salvation occurrence by demanding faith, putting to each of us the question whether we are willing to understand ourselves as crucified with Christ and as thereby also risen with him. In the sounding forth of the word, cross and resurrection become present and the eschatological now takes place. The eschatological promise of Isa. 49:8 is fulfilled: "Behold, now is the acceptable time; behold, now is the day of salvation" (2 Cor. 6:2). For this reason judgment takes place in the preaching of the apostle, who to one is "a fragrance from death to death," to the other "a fragrance from life to life" (2 Cor. 2:16). So, too, the resurrection life is at work in the faith mediated by his preaching (2 Cor. 4:12). And of the sermon that preaches Christ, the word of the Johannine Jesus holds good: "Truly, truly, I say to you, he who hears my word and believes him who sent me, has eternal life; he does not come into judgment, but has passed from death to life. . . . The hour is coming and now is when the dead will hear the voice of the Son of God and those who hear will live" (John 5:24–25). In the preached word, and only in it, is the risen one to be encountered. "Thus faith comes from what is heard, and what is heard comes by the preaching of Christ" (Rom. 10:17).

Just as the word and the apostle who preaches it belong to the eschatological occurrence, so also does the church in which the word continues to be proclaimed and within which believers gather as those who are "holy," that is, as those who have made the transition to eschatological existence. "Church" (ἐκκλησία) is an eschatological concept, and when it is called the "body of Christ," this is to express its "cosmic" meaning: it is not a historical phenomenon in the sense of world history but in the sense that it is in history that it is realized.

Conclusion

We have sought to carry out the demythologizing of the New Testament proclamation. Is there still a mythological remainder? For anyone who speaks of mythology as soon as there is any talk of God's act, of God's decisive eschatological act, there certainly is. But such mythology is no longer mythology in the old sense, so that it would have now become obsolete with the passing away of the mythical world picture. For the salvation occurrence about which we talk is not some miraculous, supernatural occurrence but rather a historical occurrence in space and time. And by presenting it as such, stripping away the mythological garments, we have intended to follow the intention of the New Testament itself and to do full justice to the paradox of its proclamation—the paradox, namely, that God's eschatological emissary is a concrete historical person, that God's eschatological act takes place in a human destiny, that it is an occurrence, therefore, that cannot be proved to be eschatological in any worldly way. It is the paradox formulated in the words "he emptied himself" (Phil. 2:7), or "he who was rich became poor" (2 Cor. 8:9), or "God sent his Son in the likeness of sinful flesh" (Rom. 8:3), or "he was manifested in the flesh" (1 Tim. 3:16), or, finally and classically, "the word became flesh" (John 1:14).

Just as he in whom God presently acts, through whom God has reconciled the world, is a real historical human being, so the word of God is not the mysterious word of some oracle but sober proclamation of the person and destiny of Jesus of Nazareth in their significance as history of salvation. As such it can be understood as a phenomenon of intellectual history and, with respect to its content of ideas, it is a possible world view; and yet this proclamation makes the claim to be the eschatological word of God.

The preachers, the apostles, are human beings who can be understood historically in their humanity. The church is a historical, sociological phenomenon, whose history can be understood historically as a part of the history of culture. And yet they are all eschatological phenomena, eschatological occurrence.

All of these claims are a "scandal" (σκάνδαλον) that is not to be overcome in philosophical dialogue but only in obedient faith. They are all phenomena that are subject to historical, sociological, and psychological examination, and yet for faith they are all eschatological phenomena. It is precisely the fact that they cannot be proved that secures the Christian proclamation against the charge that it is mythology. The transcendence of God is not made immanent as it is in myth; rather, the paradox of the presence of the transcendent God in history is affirmed: "the word became flesh."

NOTES

1. Certainly, one can say that there are persons today whose confidence in the traditional scientific world picture has been shaken, as well as others whose primitiveness qualifies them for an age of mythological thinking. Certainly, there is superstition on every hand. But a faith in spirits and wonders that has sunk to the level of superstition is something completely different from what it once was as a faith. The question is not what ideas and speculations are present here and there in unstable minds nor even to what extent an antiscientific attitude has become prevalent under the domination of slogans. The question is what world picture people actually live in. This, however, is determined by science, and it dominates us through the school, the press, the radio, the movies, and technology generally.

2. One thinks of Paul Schütz's observations about how mythical religion died out in the Orient as a result of modern hygienic and medical equipment.

3. See G. Krüger, *Einsicht und Leidenschaft, Das Wesen des platonischen Denkens* (1939), 11–12.

4. Ibid., 17–18, 56–57.

5. Thus, myth is spoken of here in the sense in which it is understood by research in the history of religions. That mode of representation is mythology in which what is unworldly and divine appears as what is worldly and human or what is transcendent appears as what is immanent, as when, for example, God's transcendence is thought of as spatial distance. Mythology is a mode of representation in consequence of which cult is understood as action in which nonmaterial forces are mediated by material means. "Myth"

is not used here, then, in that modern sense in which it means nothing more than ideology.

6. On the critical interpretation of myth, see also the important discussion of the hermeneutical structure of dogma in H. Jonas, *Augustin und das paulinische Freiheitsproblem* (1930), 66–76.

7. Adolf von Harnack, *Das Wesen des Christentums* (1905), 40, 36.

8. See, for example, E. Troeltsch, *Die Bedeutung der Geschichtlichkeit Jesu für den Glauben* (1911).

9. Hans Jonas, *Gnosis und spätantiker Geist, Die mythologische Gnosis* (1934).

10. One thinks of expressions like "the spirit of the times" or "the spirit of technology."

11. *Briefwechsel zwischen Wilhelm Dilthey und dem Grafen Paul Yorck von Wartenburg 1877–1897* (1923), 154.

12. Ibid., 158.

13. Ibid.

14. Wilhelm Kamlah, *Christentum und Selbstbehauptung* (1940), 321.

15. Ibid., 326.

16. Ibid., 335.

17. Ibid., 337.

18. Ibid., 403.

19. Ibid., 326.

20. Ibid., 337.

21. Ibid., 341, 353, 298, 330.

22. Ibid., 358.

23. Besides, Paul never uses the formula ἄφεσις τῶν ἁμαρτιῶν, which subsequently appears in the Deutero-Pauline literature (Col. 1:14; Eph. 1:7).

24. Kamlah, *Christentum und Selbstbehauptung* (1940), 353.

25. With these and the following comments I also intend to reply to the questions and reservations about me that have been voiced by Paul Althaus in *Die Wahrheit des kirchlichen Osterglaubens* (2d ed., 1941), 90ff. See my review of E. Hirsch, *Die Auferstehungsgeschichten und der christliche Glaube* (1940) in *Theologische Literaturzeitung* 65 (1940): 242–46.

THEOLOGY AS SCIENCE

(1941)

This theme requires us, first of all, to define what science is. Because we are asking whether theology in its distinctiveness is a science, and because we have to say, therefore, to what extent and in what way it is a science, we first have to define what science is.*

I

Science clearly is an idea that characterizes the procedure of individual sciences. Every science has to do with illuminating system-

*The rest of the published text follows an explicit outline that its editor, Erich Dinkler, reconstructed from the essay itself. Although I have chosen to omit the outline from the translation, which follows the typescript on which the text is based in expressly distinguishing only between sections I and II, I offer the outline here for whatever help it may be in analyzing the structure of the essay:
  I. The Concept of Science
  II. Theology as Science
    A. Its Object
      1. God as the Object of Theology
        a) The Impossibility of Objectifying God
        b) Religion as Its Object
        c) Orthodoxy
        d) Conclusion
      2. God's Eschatological Act as the Object of Theology
        a) Faith and What It Believes in as Object
        b) The Eschatological Act of God Objectified as Theme
    B. Its Procedure
      1. As New Testament Theology
      2. As Systematic Theology
      3. As Old Testament Theology
      4. As the Study of Church History
      5. As Practical Theology
  III. The Scientific Character of Theology

atically some special field of objects or subject matter to which we as human beings have access through our existence; this work of illuminating or disclosing takes place in accordance with methods called for by the objects in question and is for the sake of knowing: the researcher seeks to see (and to show to others) what is really the case with the subject matter, how it really is in its field of objects. This has a number of implications.

To speak of a field of objects is to indicate that the researcher stands over against the subject matter; it is given precisely as an object, as becomes particularly clear when even human beings can be made the object of science. We ourselves thereby become an object, and this is the objectifying procedure of science. The researcher assumes a distance from the object, which thereby stands still, so to speak, no longer being moved by the researcher's interest. (It is a modern problem whether the object ever really stands still or whether it is always influenced by research and experiment.)

Such standing over against the object is a way of simply seeing it, not a way of practically shaping it or somehow making use of it. It is the kind of seeing ($\theta \epsilon \omega \rho \epsilon \hat{\imath} \nu$) that seeks to see the subject matter as it is in itself, thereby excluding any purpose or interest. Thus, it is not the kind of aesthetic viewing that has to do with how things look and the impression they make. Rather, it is the kind of seeing that seeks to understand the object for what it is, in terms of its own inner structure, so that the individual phenomenon can be understood to be necessary in terms of the whole. This is why scientific statements not only describe but also justify. Science speaks with reasons, not, as in the case of the kerygma, with authority. Nor does it speak like the confession that subjects itself to such authority by responding to it. Such, then, is the objective procedure of science.

But to describe its procedure is not to describe its historical origin or its place in a particular culture in which either it or its results can be used for certain purposes. Science places its results, its knowledge of a particular field, at the disposal of practical interests. There can also be practical necessities that (continually even as in its origin) draw its attention to still existing obscurities and questions. Science's own real interest, however, is not practical utility but seeing things disinterestedly. And its logical (as distinct from its historical) origin is just such disinterested seeing, which in turn, of course, also rests on a human interest. Because it belongs essentially to human existence to understand itself, and because, finding itself in its world, existence attains to self-understanding in unity with understanding its world, existence as such is interested in understanding the world and hence in pure knowledge. To what extent this self-understanding intended in the knowledge of objects is active in a particular science can vary considerably. The drive to know can degenerate into mere curiosity, play, or routine; it can also combine with a drive to view things aesthetically or can be more or less suppressed by such a drive.

That scientific seeing is disinterested need not mean that it does not see its objects in their possible significance. But the significance perceived by science is not the significance of the objects for the particular person who sees them, but rather the significance they have for the whole field of objects that happens to be in question. If this field is history, the objectivity of seeing is misunderstood if the question about specific historical significance is excluded as subjective and history is understood by analogy with nature. In the study of nature any question about the significance of a particular phenomenon is found to be subjective, because significance for specifically human existence is not involved. But significance for human existence belongs to the essence of a historical object. Scientific interpretation of Plato, for example, understands the Platonic dialogues only when it understands them to have to do with the same human existence that also belongs to the interpreter. Scientific study of history, however, dims one's own vital interest or distances itself therefrom; it makes the significance of the historical phenomenon as such the object of its study.

The objectivity of science is evident in its not being interested in particular results of its research. Any result is equally good, for any result means knowledge of the object as it really is, and to see precisely this is the aim of science. It seeks nothing except to allow the object as such to show itself and to find expression.

This attitude of being disinterested in its results is usually described by saying that science is without presuppositions or, better, without prejudices. If scientific work may not presuppose any specific results, it is nevertheless possible at all only on the basis of certain presuppositions. Any science presupposes a prescientific relation to its object in which a certain understanding of the object is already included.

Science does not disclose fields of objects to which life has no relation at all but only those within which life is always already lived. In any association with a part of the world, some understanding is always already given. This understanding becomes intentional in science, in which it is developed, expanded, corrected, and justified. The knowledge of science can remain genuine, however, only if it does not lose its original life relation to its object.

This means, for instance, that the science of history is appropriate only if the historian has a relation to the subject matter with which history is concerned and if this very relation guides his or her historical understanding. To want to exclude this relation to the subject matter, as was the case under the hegemony of positivism, means to abandon history as its own field of objects and to reduce the science of history to the science of nature.

It belongs to being without presuppositions that every science stands only on its own presuppositions, which grow out of its particular field of objects, and that the presuppositions of one field (such as natural science) may not be carried over to another (such as the science of history).*

Precisely because science develops the understanding that is given in a particular relation to some subject matter, it differentiates itself into various sciences, each of which has its own field of objects. Correspondingly, each of these sciences has its own method, that is, both its own kind of conceptuality (for example, natural scientific or historical) and its own way of showing its objects and justifying its statements. Common to all sciences is the method of the λόγον διδόναι, of speaking in statements that are justified, that disclose their object in that they allow one to understand the individual part in terms of an understanding of the whole.

We shall not consider here whether or how there is a science that, for its part, makes all science the object of its research—an ency-

---

*In the text this one-sentence paragraph comes before the two paragraphs now preceding it in the translation. But for at least two reasons this can hardly be the correct order. This one-sentence paragraph evidently presupposes the point made in the opening sentence of the first of the two preceding paragraphs, that is, the sentence, "This attitude of being disinterested in its results is usually described by saying that science is without presuppositions or, better, without prejudices." And this same opening sentence, in turn, so closely follows on the closing sentence of the paragraph now preceding it as to make their being separated by an intervening paragraph extremely unlikely.

clopedia of science—and, correspondingly, whether or how there is a science that seeks to know not individual fields of objects but beings as a whole in their being—philosophy. Because we are asking about theology as science, it is sufficient to orient ourselves to what is common to all science.

In summary, science is the disclosure of a field of objects, which we may characterize more precisely as follows:

1. It is an objectifying procedure.

2. It is objective in that it sees any of its objects as a whole and in its inner structure disinterestedly and without prejudices.

3. It is rooted in a prescientific relation to its objects and develops the understanding that is given in this relation in a methodical way.

4. It has its own special method depending on its particular field of objects.

II

To what extent can theology qualify as a science, or in what way does the idea of science find expression in it? If it is a science it must disclose some field of objects by means of justified statements and in this way allow its objects to be seen in their inner structure.

The first question, clearly, must be as to the object of theology. According to both the meaning of the word "theology" and the tradition of the ancient and the medieval church, this object is God. But can God be the object of a science?

In the usual descriptions of God as otherworldly, invisible, incomprehensible, etc., the thought is expressed that God cannot be an object of human seeing, that God cannot be objectified. And the reason for this is not simply that this field of objects is quantitatively too encompassing. Other fields of science such as nature and history also cannot be encompassed. But it is the essence of God not to be encompassed, because God encompasses everything else. God does not stand still, so to speak, for seeing, because even in human seeing it is God who sees, provided God is omnipotent. God is not at the disposal of a seeing that is outside of God, for there is no outside of God. Thus, seeing God cannot be objective. Any seeing of God that would be interested only in the seeing would not be a seeing *of God*; for a seeing of God that did not see God's significance, and specifically God's significance for me as the one doing the seeing, would not be a seeing of God, who cannot be seen at all except as the one who demands and judges, gives and shows mercy, precisely in relation to me. There is knowledge of God only as existential knowing. There is theoretical knowledge not of God but only of the idea of God.

And does theology consist in working out an understanding of God that is given to human beings simply as such in their association with God, a prescientific understanding that they already have in their relation to God? Such a theology, in any case, would not be Christian theology; for Christian faith disputes the claim that human existence originally stands in association with God and claims instead that human existence is godless and is brought to knowledge of God only by God's act. God is "revealed," that is, is not in some way always already to be seen. But where God is revealed, God is revealed completely—not in a quantitative sense, for even in revelation God is "hidden," but in the sense that God is completely God in what God now says. The deity of God is not a field that can be made ever more accessible through further discoveries, so that the individual phenomenon becomes understandable in its necessity by being placed in its context in the whole. God is revealed ever anew and ever completely, that is, God's word always has utter clarity and utter authority.

It may indeed be said that even by nature human existence has a relation to God. But this can be said only from the standpoint of faith. When faith judges that human existence is by nature godless, it thereby asserts a relation to God. For this godlessness is not a privative specification, as it is when one says that an animal, a plant, or a stone is godless.* That one is godless as a human being does not mean that one is without God but rather that one has lost the God whom one simply has to have. But that one has to have God means that human existence asks the question about God and is always moved by this question. Still, that human existence asks the question about God does not mean that it has God. It does indeed have the concept of God, and this concept can also be clarified and developed scientifically. But this again makes clear that theology is not science of God, for such knowledge of the concept of God is knowledge only of

*The translation of this sentence follows the typescript on which the text is based rather than the text itself, which mistakenly reads "private" instead of "privative."

the human being who asks the question about God, and so is in no way a theological science of God.

But if God is not the object of theology as science, is its object, perhaps, faith in God? Such faith certainly seems to be a phenomenon of human life or of intellectual history that is capable of being objectified. But what is faith as such a phenomenon except religion? And what is Christian faith except a special form of the phenomenon of religion?

As a matter of fact, in the course of the nineteenth century and by the beginning of the twentieth, theology became essentially the science of religion. The biblical sciences became branches of the history of religion, and the same was true of church history insofar as it did not become simply profane history. Systematic theology became the philosophy or psychology of religion (Ernst Troeltsch and Rudolf Otto), and practical theology was now simply religious folklore, psychology of religion, and education.

This kind of theology speaks of faith on the presupposition that the object of faith is inaccessible to scientific research. Thus, it speaks of believing, not of what is believed in, of the *fides qua creditur*, not of the *fides quae creditur*. What Christian faith believes in has to become secondary. One observes that religion is always and everywhere objectified in certain ideas of God, the world, and human existence and that dogmas are everywhere the "exponent" of religious life. Insofar as they involve assertions about the world and human existence, they fall under the competence of science, which gradually dissolves them or provides a new justification for them. All that is original and indissoluble in religion is religious feeling, whose object is indefinable or is described simply as the mysterious ground of life and the world.

How can such a science of religion legitimate itself as Christian theology? It sees its task as twofold. In the first place, it seeks to show that religion develops to its highest and purest form in Christian faith. Purified of fear and superstition, religion is unmixed with science and therefore can be combined with a scientific picture of the world as a pious feeling of trust and submission in relation to the world and destiny, of a piece with the consciousness of moral responsibility. Thus, it is to be defined with Friedrich Schleiermacher as the feeling of absolute dependence, in which one is conscious at once of dependence and freedom, finitude and eternity; or with Rudolf Otto as the numinous feeling, or creature feeling, that becomes aware of the *tremendum* and the *fascinosum* of deity. In the second place, this theology seeks to prove by arguments from the philosophy of religion that, because religion rests on a "religious *a priori*," it necessarily belongs to human existence and thus also to human culture (Troeltsch).

But human beings who are moved by the question about God as well as Christians who hear the word of proclamation want to be oriented concerning the *fides quae creditur*, not their own *fides qua creditur*. They do not want to know whether theirs is the relatively highest religion or whether it has an indispensable function in human culture. They want to know whether what they believe in is true, or, alternatively, what they may and should believe in.

But this shows that religion (as well as Christian faith) is misunderstood in its own intention if it is viewed apart from its relation to its object. From the outset its meaning is that it is a relation to a certain object, namely, God. The Christian faith is what it is as *fides qua creditur* only in relation to the *fides quae creditur*. Plato already recognized that "love" (ἔρως) is always "love of something" (ἔρως τινός) and that what "love" is can be understood only when its object is understood together with it.

So, too, what religion or Christian faith is can be understood only when at the same time the object of religion, or what faith believes in, is understood together with it.

Does this mean, then, that the object of theology is God as the object of faith, as the *fides quae creditur*? It does, indeed. But there is danger here of a new misunderstanding, to which orthodoxy has succumbed. It rightly sees that a theology that is nothing but the science of religion surrenders the *fides quae creditur* that it as orthodoxy wishes to uphold. But it thereby abandons or falsifies the *fides qua creditur*.

For orthodoxy the *fides quae creditur* is right teaching, whose truth is proved partly by reason, partly by scripture, in other words, partly by proofs that are rationally evident, partly by proofs that can be believed only by submitting *ratio* to the authority of scripture (whose authority is in turn established by a kind of proof). In this way the statements comprising the *fides quae creditur* acquire the character of general truths, that is, truths that are valid apart from any existential relation to the concrete situation of the speaker, hence truths that are not visible only in and for faith but rather are developed prior to faith, to which the believer must then give assent. This misunderstanding of the *fides qua creditur* comes to light in the Protestant orthodox doctrine according to which *assensus (generalis)*, as the second part of faith following upon *notitia*, precedes *fiducia*.

This attitude of orthodoxy also appears both in its natural theology and in its doctrine of the inspiration of scripture. According to this doctrine, the statements of scripture are general truths that one has to accept even when one cannot see them to be true, and so God's revelation is not understood as occurring *in actu* but is thought of as God's having already been revealed. The orthodox attitude is also apparent, once its doctrine of scripture is shaken by the science of history, in its resistance against historical criticism of scripture, its frantic attempts to prove authenticity, and so on.

If the *fides qua creditur* is viewed as assent to a *fides quae creditur*, itself understood as a sum of doctrines that one is supposed to believe, but to which one would never come on one's own and which one could hold to be true only by a partial if not total *sacrificium intellectus*, then the *fides qua creditur* has become a human work, a decision to accept claims as true that are not evident in themselves. But such a faith is in no way related to God as its object; one cannot believe in a doctrine but can only hold it to be "credible" or "incredible," right or wrong. If one imagines one can believe in it, faith becomes merely the decision to hold it to be true.

Both liberalism and orthodoxy, then, have lost the object of theology. By making the *fides qua creditur* its only object, liberalism loses what faith believes in, without which it cannot be understood. Orthodoxy, on the other hand, loses the *fides qua creditur* because it supposes it has the *fides quae creditur*. The *fides qua creditur* can be understood only in its relation to the *fides quae creditur*, and, correspondingly, the *fides quae creditur* can be understood only in its relation to the *fides qua creditur*. Only so is the *fides quae creditur* even visible, the *fides qua creditur* being the sole possibility of access to it. Were it otherwise, and were it possible for there to be a theology prior to the *fides qua creditur*, such faith would be unnecessary. Its object would no longer be the *fides quae creditur* but only that theology to which *assensus* is the proper response and on which it has to rely.

The task of theology, then, must be determined by its object, given the sole possible mode of access thereto. What God is cannot be understood unless what faith is is also understood—and conversely. Theology, therefore, is the science of God in that it is at the same time the science of faith—and conversely. Thus, the object of theology is faith itself in unity with what it believes in.

But faith and its object cannot be seen in their unity from any standpoint outside of faith—for example, in the way in which one can see a marksman taking aim without taking aim oneself, even though the marksman can be understood as such only if his target is also seen (or understood), and the target can be understood as a target only by also seeing the marksman. On the contrary, if God is visible only to faith, faith, also, is visible only to faith. Therefore, theology is a movement of faith in which faith understands itself.

Faith knows God not in God's being in itself but in God's acting on us. It knows that even it itself as faith is what it is only through God's act. It knows that it is at all only because it is not from itself, that it is not freely constituted as an independent human attitude by its own decision in the way in which science and art are. It knows that it is created by what it believes in. For this reason the ground and the object of faith are identical (Wilhelm Herrmann).

And, to be sure, faith knows itself to be created by the word of scripture, which encounters it in the church's proclamation as word of God. In scripture it is told that God is revealed in Christ in such a way that through Christ God has judged the world and brought forth a new world in which everyone may have a part who believes in God's act in Christ, that is, who allows it to happen to his or her own existence. In the proclaiming word and in the faith that is open to this word, God's act in Christ continues to take place and, therefore, is precisely not a past historical event under whose impact we still live but rather is the "eschatological" occurrence. It is visible only to the very faith to which it itself occurs. Faith is not taking notice of an event of the past that is mediated by historical tradition but rather itself belongs to the eschatological occurrence by virtue of the proclamation in which this occurrence continues to take place.

As an eschatological phenomenon faith is complete conversion from the world to God, from being forsaken by God to the grace of God. Believers know themselves to be "a new creation" (καινὴ κτίσις), to be "born again." And they know of their regeneration only in faith and cannot establish it in itself by demonstrable new qualities. Theirs is faith in justification: *simul iustus, simul peccator.*

Faith, then, is not a special mode of knowledge, an organ by which otherwise invisible objects or states of affairs might be perceived, but rather, as itself belonging to the eschatological occurrence, is a mode of existing, of existing in faith in and from the history of salvation.

This faith is itself the theme of theology. But it can become the theme of theology only if it is at the same time the motive of theology. For faith is conscious that any other motivation would fall outside of it, that any knowing of faith that is not motivated by faith itself would surrender faith, which can understand itself only believingly.

Theology is possible, therefore, only as a movement of believing existence itself and cannot be justified as correct or necessary in terms of a system of the sciences projected outside of faith or on the basis of culture. Theology makes sense and is justified only if it is grounded in faith itself, that is, only if it actualizes believing existence, only if faith confirms and develops itself in it, only, therefore, if it belongs essentially to the eschatological occurrence, which continues to take place in it.

The theme of theology, then, is the eschatological occurrence in which God is seen as the one who acts on us and effects faith and we are seen as those who are thereby drawn into God's action.

Because this occurrence is interpreted scientifically, that is, in concepts and justified statements, it is objectified. And so the paradox seems to happen that the theologian assumes an objectifying distance toward his or her own faith, that, motivated by faith, he or she takes up a standpoint outside of faith. Is this possible?

At first glance nothing may seem to happen here other than what always happens when believers elsewhere in life obey the duties of the situation and of the moment. They have to fulfill such duties as believers, and yet they can only believe that they fulfill them as believers. They cannot see their own faith, cannot be conscious of acting in faith, but can only believe it.

But is it not really different in the case of theology from our action otherwise? In all other action what to do and to what end are given in the concrete situation. Thus it is in so-called practical action, which has to do what is necessary in the moment. The farmer, the artisan, the technician, the physician, and the homemaker are required to act by the concrete situation, and while they are to carry out their action in a Christian way, what they are to do and the end to which they are to do it are not given by what is Christian. The same is true of the theoretical action of science, which is likewise called for by the situation. Indeed, even for theology there is such a requirement arising out of the concrete situation, in that theology is called for by the situation of the church and of the world.

But is there not a distinctive difference between theological work and all other kinds of work? Of course, all action should take place from faith and in faith, and because faith is present only in existing, one can also say that any believing action is by way of developing faith, which exists only insofar as it is somehow developed. Nevertheless, in the case of all other kinds of action the development of faith is not the conscious purpose of the action, and it cannot be so if faith is to remain faith and not become a work. Faith is the genuine motive of action when action is purely matter-of-fact, that is, when it is determined by the situation that calls for my action and demands my devotion. I act believingly only when I act devotedly—in love— and thus only when I act for the sake of the other person, not when I act in order to develop my faith. In fact, can faith be developed at all if it is made the object of pure seeing, in the way in which theology seeks to do?

Even theology acts matter-of-factly if it knows itself called for by the questions of the world or by the difficulties and needs of the church. But it seems to become something other than matter-of-fact even in its matter-of-factness if it makes the development of faith itself its aim. In it faith reflects on itself and proves itself, not simply as in all other action but by making itself the object of pure seeing. And by becoming distant to itself, it risks itself. It halts, as it were, in the midst of its own movement and asks, What am I doing when I believe? Can I, may I, believe? And with this it is already unfaith. This is the paradox of theology, that as a movement of faith itself it should halt in its movement, that, believing, it should not believe. How is such an attitude possible and justified?

It is possible, justified, and necessary because faith is faith in justification, because it is faith in the grace of God that justifies the sinner. For this means that the new eschatological existence of the believer does not become a quality that is present and can be disposed of but rather that unbelieving existence prior to faith is sublated in it, being preserved even as overcome. Paul forgets what lies behind him, not in the sense that he puts it out of mind but in the sense that it is present to him as overcome by God (Phil. 3:13). He recalls it quite intensively in order to become conscious of the present or, better, in order to become conscious of the future that lies ahead of him. He has no abiding present, and he knows himself to live from the future only because he knows himself as the one who comes out of his past.

In faith in justification believers are given a new understanding of themselves in unity with a new understanding of the word of God to which faith is the answer. The new self-understanding has to prove its newness over against the old self-understanding, even as Paul does this in Phil. 3:3ff. To be sure, this new self-understanding can be present in an unreflective form. But it is constantly in danger of slipping back into a natural self-understanding, whether legalistic, naturalistic, or idealistic. Theology is nothing other than the reflective, methodical unfolding of the understanding of the word of God and of the self-understanding disclosed through this word and given in faith.

Faith thus contains undeveloped theology because it is an understanding faith, just as any practical human attitude toward one's fellow human beings and the world, toward one's own life and destiny, is sustained by an understanding that is capable of being unfolded theoretically and is in need of being thus unfolded. In fact, the very existence of such competing world views demands an explication of the self-understanding of faith.

This means, however, that it belongs to the very essence of faith that it can stand outside itself, indeed, that it must do so. Because faith is a gift, not a work or a possession, it needs to stand outside of itself so that it becomes conscious of the gift as gift. It needs to reflect on itself, and it is in just this way that it becomes conscious of the full seriousness of what faith means. But this it can do only if it becomes distant from itself, by asking, Why do I believe? Can I, may I, believe? What happens when I believe? Theology develops just these questions—not, indeed, in order to assure itself that faith makes sense and is justified from some outside standpoint (such as that of a profane science or philosophy), thereby justifying faith before the forum of existence outside of faith, but rather in order to become conscious of the meaning of faith by placing existence outside of faith before the forum of faith.

Thus, theology is necessarily given with faith as faith in justification. And theology is also necessary for the community so that knowledge of the meaning of faith in justification is not buried under in it.

Still one must ask whether the theology that is thus necessary is properly a science that can only be undertaken systematically. Is not such reflection as belongs to the essence of faith a matter for every believer, and is it not enough that there is the preaching of the community, which can just as well be taken over by lay believers who have no need of theological science?

Indeed so, one could reply—at any rate, in principle. But one may very well doubt whether the preaching of the community always fulfills this task in an appropriate way. And one can then say that there is a certain security for the church if there are believers who can engage in such reflection consciously and as a matter of vocation. But there is even more to be said.

Theology is necessary because faith as faith in justification is related to its ground. Its ground, however, is the eschatological act of God which is not evident as an act in world history but rather takes place in the proclamation through which faith is evoked and in which it believes. Theology as science has the task of securing this proclamation.

This proclamation does not present general truths that are eternally valid and that must be justified by thinking but rather speaks of the act of God which has occurred in a certain history and through which it acquires its legitimation. Thus, the task is set of interpreting the New Testament, the document in which this history is attested, and theology assumes the task. Consequently, theology does not "teach" in the sense in which philosophy "teaches" when philosophy seeks the truth and, to the extent that it thinks it has found the truth, "teaches" it. Theology, on the contrary, in a certain sense already has the truth in the proclamation of the New Testament. In philosophy, science and teaching are identical, and the right philosophy itself would be right teaching. Theology, by contrast, "teaches" what the New Testament "teaches." It "teaches" what "right teaching" is, that is, it interprets the New Testament, and this means, in the first place, it translates the New Testament.

But translating the New Testament calls for scientific work, not only because any translation is imperfect and needs to be revised critically by reference to the original text but above all because even the most accurate translation itself needs to be translated in the next generation. Language is alive and has its own history. Conceptualities change, and scientific study of the New Testament has the task of translating the text into the language of each particular present and into its conceptuality.

Even this task is not merely philological-historical but also theological. Or, better, just as in being a theological task it is also philological-historical, so in being a philological-historical task it is also theological. This is so because the philological-historical interpretation of any historical document (as only positivism can deny) presupposes a relation between the interpreter and the particular subject matter that is involved. Just as only a mathematician can explain a document of ancient mathematics, and a musician or musical person a document in the history of music, so only a philosopher can appropriately interpret Plato, and only a scholar moved by the question of faith can interpret the New Testament.

But the theological character of the scientific interpretation of the New Testament can be understood even more definitely. Since the proclamation does not simply proclaim propositions or a dogma but an act of God in history, and since this act of God as eschatological act is not simply evident as an event of world history but is grasped as such only in faith, it can never be presented independently of the eyes of faith but only as faith sees it and as it finds expression in believing existence and its whole attitude toward life.

Naturally, certain dogmatic statements can be abstracted from the New Testament, which expresses the Christ occurrence in mythological form. But if they are understood without also understanding what happens in this occurrence to anyone affected by it, and thus what happens in faith as well as in unfaith, then they are pure myth, just like the myth of any mystery deity. Thus, the formulation of the kerygma, which is formulated by a believing human being and not by an angel, always arises out of the believing self-understanding of the proclaimer and is cast in the conceptuality of his or her time. The self-understanding can be more or less developed and can differentiate itself according to the historical situation. Thus, in the New Testament a series of differentiated kerygmatic formulations appear which in Paul or in John are conditioned by opposition to Jewish legalism or Gnosticism.

(The statements of scripture cannot be taken over as doctrinal laws, for God's revelation does not mean that God has already been revealed, that is, God is not directly given in revelation, which is present only *in actu*, as occurrence, an occurrence that cannot be observed like other happenings in the world but is perceivable only by one who participates in it. It is seen only in faith which itself participates in it, and so the faith of the New Testament also is not distinguished simply by dogmatic statements, which are themselves only the expression of believing existence in its particular situation. But, naturally, this occurrence is also not present in the experiences of persons of the New Testament, so that study of the New Testament would have the task of presenting the religious lives of these persons instead of presenting statements of faith.*)

Interpretation of the New Testament, then, has to inquire back behind the different formulations in order to construct, so to speak, an ideal type of the kerygma. But it at once becomes clear that there neither is nor can be any such ideal type. And this is so because, given the nature of the eschatological occurrence, one cannot perceive it at all except by being drawn into it; this means that any particular formulation is determined by the extent and direction of development of the believer's self-understanding and by the conceptuality of the time. Consequently, what a scholar today might be able to establish as the unifying meaning of the New Testament kerygma would be formulated for today, and only for today. But this explains at once both the direction and the urgency of New Testament research.

So far as its direction is concerned, interpretation of the New Testament can only be critical in the sense that it measures the theological formulations of the New Testament by their own subject matter, that

---

*The translation here reverses the order in the text of this and the preceding sentence.

is, by asking to what extent the eschatological occurrence of which faith knows by participating in it finds its legitimate expression in the theological formulations. Thus arises the peculiar paradox that research can acquire its understanding of the subject matter, of the eschatological occurrence, only from the witnesses of the New Testament and yet at the same time is critical of these same witnesses. It is bound to these witnesses and yet also free from them, being freed from them precisely through them themselves.

This Christian freedom even in being bound to tradition is given essentially in the fact that God's eschatological act takes place in history, and thus in the fact that "the word became flesh."

Just as clear is the urgency of New Testament research: it has to work out for the community the formulation of the kerygma that is appropriate today. In doing this it competes in every way with systematic theology.

What meaning does systematic theology have alongside of New Testament theology? If it is to be legitimate theology, it, too, can only be the systematic explication of the Christian understanding of existence given in faith. In other words, its task cannot be to develop the statements of Christian faith as so many general truths, to order them in a system, and then to offer a proof for the truth of this system on the basis of the philosophy of religion. Even systematic theology has to speak, not of God's being in itself but of God's eschatological acting on us. Thus, it does not have to be the kind of dogmatics that develops doctrines of God, of human existence, and of Christ in individual loci, only to add yet further loci on redemption and, finally, on "last things." On the contrary, the whole of dogmatics has to be eschatology, that is, an explication of God's act as eschatological act. In this way it deals with God and at the same time with Christ, in whom God's eschatological act takes place.

But how, then, is it distinguished from New Testament theology? The latter interprets the New Testament; therefore, it has as its materials the assertions of a Christian understanding of existence during New Testament times, together with kerygmatic formulations that point back to a unified kerygma; and on this basis it has to reconstruct such a unified kerygma (in the sense previously explained). Systematic theology proceeds in the reverse direction from the kerygma proclaimed in the church today, from the church's present action (for example, even from the worship life in Alpirsbach),* which, if it does not want to remain merely a show, has to be interpreted theologically. The New Testament kerygma is made present not only by being interpreted through scientific research but also by the proclamation and action of the church. Therefore, systematic theology proceeds in the reverse way from New Testament theology in that it has to unfold the Christian understanding of existence by beginning with the present kerygma.

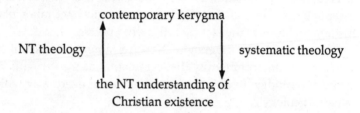

But since the kerygma today acquires its legitimation from the Christ event of the past, present preaching and systematic theology with it have need of a critical control that secures its identity with the apostolic preaching—namely, New Testament theology. And New Testament theology, in turn, has need of present preaching and systematic theology as a control—not, to be sure, so that a contemporary dogmatics could prescribe the results of its research but rather so that it can ask the question posed by the kerygma. The relation to the subject matter that in other sciences is given to the researcher by human existence as such is given to the student of the New Testament only through contemporary proclamation, because the subject matter here is the eschatological act of . God. The church mediates the New Testament as God's word, so that it is not only a document of the history of religion but is heard by the student in its present (that is, eschatological) claim. If the believing understanding of existence expressed in the New Testament is to be understood as a live possibility today, the present must be affected in the same way as the past by the kerygma by reference to which it understands the past as a believing past. Were there no contemporary

*Alpirsbach was the site of the theological conference at which this essay was to have been read as the second of Bultmann's two contributions, the first being "New Testament and Mythology."

church with its preaching and dogmatics, the student of the New Testament would not understand the reference of faith to the kerygma but would take faith to be a religious attitude arising out of existence itself and the kerygma to be only a myth, which he or she would critically eliminate.

So it is that the relation of systematic theology and the scientific interpretation of the New Testament to one another is grounded in the uniqueness of Christian faith or in the uniqueness of the eschatological occurrence that is grasped by faith and continues in it. There must be both scientific study of the New Testament and systematic theology because God has acted in history in such a way that the act begun in Christ is the eschatological act, that is, an act that puts an end to world history and grounds a new history of human beings who exist in faith, and also because this history continues or, better, remains ever present in the proclamation and in the faith that responds to it, and because the proclamation goes back to the New Testament.

Thus, the theme of New Testament theology is fundamentally the same as that of systematic theology: the conceptual explication of Christian self-understanding, or of the eschatological occurrence, as it is attested in faith for faith. New Testament theology explicates this occurrence by interpreting the New Testament in such a way that the present urgency of the occurrence can be understood. Systematic theology explicates this occurrence as it is attested in the present in such a way that this present occurrence can be understood as the occurrence attested in the New Testament.

This, however, is to describe the inner meaning of New Testament and systematic theology, not the technique of their ways of working. The urgency of scientific study of the New Testament need not be expressed by talking about its urgency and by offering up-to-date formulations. On the other hand, the appropriateness of dogmatics to scripture need not be evidenced by proof texts and by supporting its claims with citations from scripture. Such citations can also be misleading in displaying an appropriateness to scripture that is merely external. The only thing that counts is identity in subject matter.

Must there also be the other traditional disciplines of theology?

Scientific study of the Old Testament is the presupposition of scientific study of the New Testament, whose language is not to be understood without a knowledge of the Old Testament. But beyond this the faith of the New Testament understands the eschatological occurrence in Christ as the fulfillment of Old Testament hope. Thus, Old Testament theology has to clarify the relation of prophecy and fulfillment (or has to work at this in collaboration with New Testament theology). Moreover, since New Testament faith understands its relation to the Old Testament as that of gospel to law, Old Testament theology has to clarify this relation as well (or has to work at doing so together with New Testament theology). Old Testament theology has to be careful, however, not to construe the history of Old Testament religion so as to try to present the so-called preparatory action of God as a phenomenon that can be proved historically, or to view the faith in God of the Old Testament as a religious phenomenon that points beyond itself. Study of the Old Testament is theology only if it interprets the Old Testament in terms of the New Testament, that is, *sub specie* the eschatological occurrence to which the New Testament bears witness.

Scientific study of church history acquires its theological character only if it, also, contributes toward illuminating the eschatological occurrence. It does this, first of all, in that by presenting the historical continuum it preserves the tradition, thereby making possible the work of translating the New Testament. For it is solely tradition that opens up access to a past historical epoch and its documents. Of course, this tradition is present (in the proclamation of the church) even without the scientific study of church history. But it is in the study of church history that it becomes conscious.

Beyond this the scientific study of church history has an essential contribution to make to interpreting the New Testament. The full meaning of a historical phenomenon is always disclosed only in the course of history. But if the ideas of Plato or Martin Luther or Johann Wolfgang von Goethe or Friedrich Hölderlin first become clear in their consequences and thus in their meaning only in ever new historical situations and in response to ever new ways of asking questions, the same can be said by analogy about the New Testament. The weight of Pauline ideas becomes all the clearer when they are viewed from the standpoint of Augustine or of Luther.

Nor is this all. If Christian proclamation always exists only *in actu* as occurrence, and if Christian faith is always present only in existing Christianly, there is neither a definitive form of Christian kerygma nor a definitive expression of Christian self-understanding, but both must always appear in an ever new form contingently upon each historical situation. Thus, in the first place, the study of church history has the critical function of preventing any petrifaction of the kerygma and of the theological interpretation of believing self-understanding, in that it exhibits what is Christian in particular formulations. At the same time it also has the critical task of exposing pseudoforms as precisely that, and to this extent it cannot dispense with the categories of right teaching and heresy. But in addition it has the positive task of clarifying the rich possibilities of existing Christianly, and thus retrospectively helping to open up an understanding of the New Testament and prospectively making faith in the present aware of what it really has. And in all of this it has to show what is really the church.

Such study does its work not by reducing the occurrence of church history to an occurrence of world history but rather by showing how the church is present in the occurrence of world history as an eschatological phenomenon visible to faith. It is evident that it can thus do its work only on the basis of a certain understanding of faith that functions for it as a criterion for understanding phenomena of church history. But for it, too, the history it would understand is also a critical control on its own understanding of faith, so that its being bound to tradition even in being free from it is analogous to that involved in the scientific study of the New Testament.

Practical theology is grounded in the fact that the eschatological occurrence takes place in the proclamation that both awakens faith and in turn arises out of it. As a consequence all theological disciplines are "practical" insofar as they show even this to be the case and thereby so develop faith as to impel it to proclamation and to equip it therefor. Practical theology in the narrower sense has the task that then arises of working out the particular form of proclamation that is appropriate. Appropriateness in this instance is oriented, on the one hand, to the present situation with its questions and interests, its limitations and opportunities, its self-understanding and conceptuality and, on the other hand, to the understanding of the proclamation worked out by historical and systematic theology.

So it is, then, that theology as science is both grounded and unfolded in its individual branches as the systematic working out of the self-understanding given in Christian faith. The scientific character of theology has to correspond to its object and cannot be judged by a standard that another science could provide. It is distinguished from every other science by the fact that its object—God's eschatological act—is not visible to existence outside of faith but only becomes visible when such an existence experiences conversion through faith. Thus, there not only is no prospect of trying to justify theology as science before the forum of an unbelieving culture, but any such effort would also mean the self-surrender of theology. The object of theology is visible only to faith, and this faith itself belongs to its object—in fact, it *is* its object in the sense that God's act, the eschatological occurrence, takes place in it itself. Consequently, the conceptuality of theology must be peculiar to it, in correspondence with its object; and so, too, with the way in which it justifies its statements by giving reasons for them. How its conceptuality is related to that of other interpretations of human existence outside of faith is a question that cannot be pursued here. It is connected with the question of how the sublation of existence prior to faith in existence in faith is to be explicated more exactly, and hence with the further question of just how we are to understand the relation to God prior to faith that appears in the question about God by which existence as such is moved.

In any case, theology is a science like all other sciences in that it stands under the demand of the λόγον διδόναι, in that it has to test its assertions and concepts by its object, and in that its formal procedure is purely rational, involving no other logic than that involved in any other science. And so all the other defining characteristics of a science also apply to it:

1. It is a science in that it is an objectifying procedure. It stands over against its object.

2. It is a science in that it is objective and seeks nothing except to see its object and, however much it may be practically motivated in its actual work, pursues no practical purposes in doing its work.

3. It is a science in that it is rooted in a prescientific relation to its object and develops the understanding given in this relation in a methodical way.

4. It is always unconcluded, and its results are relative.

5. Its results can be preserved.

6. It has its own method which corresponds to its field of objects.

The first three of these characteristics, however, define theology in a peculiarly paradoxical way:

1. The object that it stands over against is it itself, insofar as it itself is a

movement of the faith that is its object, such faith being included in the eschatological occurrence that must be considered its proper object.

2. Although it is objective and is interested only in seeing its object, still, because it itself is the attitude of faith, it is at the same time subjectivity. Once again, however, this is not so in the way in which the attitude of objectivity can become subjectivity in any science if it becomes an end in itself. Rather, it is so because the subjectivity in question is not that of human existence relating itself to itself but precisely that in which it relates itself to God, so that its γινώσκειν is a γνωσθῆναι.

3. It is rooted in a prescientific understanding of its object insofar as faith itself is always already understanding. But its object is not given to human existence as such, but rather is first disclosed to it only with that conversion of human existence which is its object.

THE PROBLEM OF HERMENEUTICS

(1950)

I

According to Wilhelm Dilthey, hermeneutics as the "art of understanding expressions of life fixed in writing" always draws attention to itself only "during a great historical movement." Such a movement makes "understanding unique historical existence," or "scientific knowledge of individual persons, in fact, of the great forms of unique human existence in general," an urgent concern of science.[1] If we today are in the midst of "a great historical movement," there is reason to consider the problem of hermeneutics. And in point of fact, discussion with the historical tradition forms an essential part of contemporary self-reflection, which is simultaneously reflection on "the great forms of unique human existence."

The problem with which hermeneutics is concerned, according to Dilthey, arises from the question, "Is such a knowledge [namely, of the great forms of unique human existence] possible, and what means do we have for attaining it?" More specifically it is the question "whether understanding the unique can be raised to the level of general validity." "How can one individual come to an objective, generally valid understanding of another individual's expression of life as given through the senses?"[2] Thus, it is the question of the possibility of achieving objectivity in understanding unique historical existence of the past. In principle, it is a question of the possibility of understanding historical phenomena in general insofar as they are witnesses to unique human existence, in which case hermeneutics would be the science of understanding history in general. In fact, Dilthey restricts hermeneutics to the interpretation of "expressions of life that are enduringly fixed," namely, monuments of culture, and so primarily literary documents, although works of art, also, are of essential importance.[3]

II

Ever since Aristotle hermeneutical rules have been developed for the interpretation of literary texts, and these rules have become traditional and are usually followed as a matter of course.[4] As Aristotle himself saw, the first requirement is for a formal analysis of a literary work with respect to its structure and style.[5] Interpretation has to analyze the composition of the work, understanding the parts in light of the whole and the whole in light of the parts. This yields the insight that any interpretation moves in a "hermeneutical circle." As soon as one undertakes to interpret texts in an ancient or foreign language, one becomes aware of the further requirement that the interpretation must be done in accordance with the rules of grammar. Already with the Alexandrians this demand for a grammatical knowledge of the language was supplemented by the demand for a knowledge of the individual author's usage, so that, for example, a criterion was acquired by means of which to decide questions of authenticity in the interpretation of Homer. With the development of historical work during the Enlightenment, the question about the individual author's usage was expanded into the question about the use of language in the particular period in which the text was written. But hand in hand with insight into the historical development of language went knowledge of historical development in general, and hence of the fact that all literary documents are historically conditioned by circumstances of time and place, which henceforth must be known if there is to be any appropriate interpretation.

The science that has as its object the interpretation of literary texts and that makes use of hermeneutics to this end is philology. In the course of its development, however, it becomes clear that hermeneutics as the art of scientific understanding is by no means adequately defined by these traditional hermeneutical rules. Harald Patzer has recently shown how philology, which began by using the science of history for the purpose of interpretation, gradually came to be used by history, or itself became the branch of history for which texts are only "witnesses" or "sources" for projecting a historical picture by reconstructing some past time.[6] This is certainly an understandable development, since there is also naturally a circle between philological and historical knowledge. But the upshot was that philology lost its real object in the interpretation of texts for the sake of understanding them. The deeper reason for this development, however, is that the task of understanding was not understood profoundly enough and thus seemed to have already been accomplished simply by following the hermeneutical rules. In other words, the insight into the process of understanding for which Friedrich Schleiermacher had once striven had been lost.

Schleiermacher had already seen that a genuine understanding cannot be achieved simply by following the hermeneutical rules. In addition to the interpretation that they serve to guide, which in his terminology is called "grammatical," there must also be "psychological" interpretation. Schleiermacher recognized that the composition and unity of a work cannot be grasped solely by the categories of a formal logical and stylistic analysis. Rather, the work must be understood as a moment in the life of a certain human being. In addition to grasping the "outer form," one must grasp the "inner form," which is a matter not of objective but of subjective, "divinatory" interpretation.[7] Thus, interpretation is a matter of "reproduction" or "reconstruction" that takes place in living relation to the process of literary production itself. Understanding becomes "one's own recreation of the living nexus of thoughts."[8] Such "recreation" is possible because "the individuality of the interpreter and that of the author do not stand over against one another as two incomparable facts." Rather, "both have been formed on the basis of universal human nature, whereby the community of human beings with one another in speech and understanding is made possible."[9] Dilthey appropriates these ideas of Schleiermacher and seeks to explain them further: "All distinctions between individuals are ultimately conditioned not by qualitative differences between one person and another but by differences of degree between their psychical processes. If as interpreters, then, we transpose our own life experimentally, as it were, into another historical milieu, we are able for the time being to stress or strengthen one psychical process, even while allowing another to recede, and thus to reproduce another alien life in ourselves." The condition of understanding "lies in the fact that nothing can appear in the expression of another individual that is not also contained in the life of the interpreter." Thus, it can be said that "interpretation is a work of personal art whose consummate exercise is conditioned by the genius of the interpreter; it rests on congeniality, intensified by living closely with the author by constant study."[10]

Schleiermacher's view of understanding is naturally connected historically with J. J. Winckelmann's "interpretation of works of art" and with J. G. von Herder's "congenial empathy with the souls of epochs and races."[11] It is oriented to the interpretation of philosophical and poetic texts. But is it also valid for other texts? Does the interpretation of a text in mathematics or medicine, say, grow out of reenacting the psychical processes that took place in the author? Or what about the inscriptions of Egyptian kings reporting their deeds in war, or the historical and chronological texts of ancient Babylonia and Assyria, or the grave inscription of Antiochus of Commagene, or the *Res Gestae Divi Augusti?* Are they, too, understandable only insofar as one transposes oneself into the inner creative process out of which they emerged?

No, it would not appear so. And in point of fact, it is not in this way that they must be understood insofar as the interpretation has to do with what they directly communicate—thus, for example, their mathematical or medical knowledge or their report of the facts and processes of world history. But this, of course, is the primary interest of those who read such texts. To be sure, even they may be read with another interest, as is shown, for example, by Georg Misch's interpretation of the inscriptions in question as "expressions of life" or "forms of unique human existence," whether of individual persons or as expressing the "feeling for life," or understanding of existence, of certain epochs.[12] It thus becomes clear that the view of Schleiermacher and Dilthey is one-sided insofar as it is guided by a certain way of asking questions.

The upshot, then, is that any understanding or interpretation is always oriented to a certain way of asking questions or to a certain objective. This means that it is never without presuppositions; more exactly, it is always guided by a preunderstanding of the subject matter about which it questions the text. Only on the basis of such a preunderstanding is a way of asking questions and an interpretation at all possible.[13]

The subject matter about which Dilthey questions texts is "life," namely, the personal, historical life that has taken shape in the texts as "expressions of life that are enduringly fixed"; it is the "psychical life" that is to be objectively known by interpretation of "expressions that are given and perceptible through the senses." But this is not the only subject matter with which interpretation can have to do; therefore, the process of understanding characterized by this interest is not the only such process that can be enacted in an interpretation. Rather, in each case the process of understanding will be different, depending on how the objective of interpretation is determined.

It is evidently not enough to say "depending on the kind of text," that is, on the subject matter that is directly expressed in the text or the interest by which it itself is guided. For all texts can in fact be interpreted in the way in which Dilthey asks questions, that is, as documents of personal, historical life. Of course, in the first instance questioning of the text is oriented to the subject matter that is talked about in the text and mediated by it. Thus, I interpret a text in the history of music by asking what it contributes to my understanding of music and its history, and so on.

III

A way of asking questions, however, grows out of an interest that is grounded in the life of the questioner; and the presupposition of all understanding interpretation is that this interest is also alive in some way in the text to be interpreted and establishes communication between the text and the interpreter. Insofar as Dilthey designates kinship between the author and the interpreter as the condition of the possibility of understanding, he does in fact discover the presupposition of all understanding interpretation. For this condition holds good not only for the special way of asking questions distinctive of Schleiermacher and Dilthey but also for any other interpretation that can never be accomplished simply by following the traditional "hermeneutical rules." All that is necessary is that this presupposition be more exactly defined. What is required instead of reflection on the individuality of the author and of the interpreter, on their psychical processes, and on the interpreter's genius or congeniality is reflection on the simple fact that the presupposition of understanding is the life relation of the interpreter to the subject matter that is—directly or indirectly—expressed in the text.[14]

Interpretation does not come about simply because "the individuality of the interpreter and that of the author do not stand over against one another as two incomparable facts" but because or insofar as both have the same life relation to the subject matter under discussion or in question. And this they have because or insofar as they both stand in the same context of life. This relation to the subject matter with which the text is concerned, or about which it is questioned, is the presupposition of understanding.[15] For this reason it is also understandable that every interpretation is guided by a certain objective, for a question that is oriented somehow is possible only because of the conditions of a context of life. It is likewise understandable for the same reason that every interpretation includes a certain preunderstanding, namely, the one growing out of the context of life to which the subject matter belongs.

The fact that underlying any interpretation there is a life relation to the subject matter with which the text is concerned, or about which it is questioned, can be readily illustrated by reflecting on the process of translating from a foreign language. The nature of this process is as a rule obscured because knowledge of ancient languages in our cultural sphere is mediated to us by tradition and does not have to be acquired anew. Knowledge of a foreign language can be acquired anew (provided there are no texts in more than one language) only when the subject matters designated by the words (things, modes of conduct, etc.) are familiar from use and association in life. An object or a way of acting that is simply meaningless in my context of life, in my environment, or in my way of living is also unintelligible and untranslatable when it is designated in language, unless a word is chosen for it that describes its outer appearance—as, for example, when the *churunga* of the Australian aborigines is rendered in German by *Schwirrholz* (literally, whirring wood).[16] Observing use, insofar as it is understandable, can lead to further descriptions, so that a *churunga* can be described as a "powerful instrument of magic," assuming that the idea of instruments of magic is intelligible to me in my own context of life. In principle, the same process is involved whenever texts are given in or with pictorial presentations that for their part can be understood in terms of my life context. In fact, a child's understanding language and learning how to speak take place together with its becoming familiar with the environment and with human associations, in short, with the context of life.

Therefore, interpretation always presupposes a life relation to the different subject matters that—directly or indirectly—come to expression in texts. I understand a text that treats of music only if and insofar as I have a relation to music, which explains why many parts of Thomas Mann's *Doktor Faustus* are unintelligible to many readers. Likewise, I understand a mathematical text only if I have a relation to mathematics or a historical account only insofar as I am familiar with life in history and know from my own living what a state is and what possibilities there are for living in a state. Finally, I understand a novel only because I know from my own life what is involved, for example, in love and friendship, family and vocation, and so on. It is for just this reason that many pieces of literature are closed to many persons, depending on their age or education.

Naturally, my life relation to the subject matter can be utterly naive and unreflective, and in the process of understanding, in the interpretation, it can be raised to the level of consciousness and clarified. It can also be superficial and ordinary, and through understanding of the text it can be deepened and enriched, modified and corrected. In any case, a life relation to the subject matter in question is presupposed, and recognizing this eliminates certain false problems right from the outset—like, for example, the question about the possibility of understanding an "alien soul." The possibility of such understanding is given simply in the common relation of author and interpreter alike to the particular subject matter. If Dilthey affirms that the condition of the possibility of understanding is a "basis of universal human nature," or the fact that "nothing can appear in the expression of another individual that is not also contained in the life of the interpreter," this can be put more precisely by saying that the condition of interpretation is the fact that interpreter and author are human beings who live in the same historical world in which human existence takes place as existence in an environment in understanding association with objects and other persons. Naturally, it belongs to such understanding association that it should also include questions and problems, struggle and suffering, joy as well as resigned withdrawal.

IV

Interest in the subject matter motivates interpretation and provides a way of asking questions, an objective. The orientation of the interpretation is not problematic when it is guided by a question concerning the subject matter that the text itself intends to communicate—as, for example, when I seek to acquire knowledge of mathematics from a mathematical text or of music from a text in musicology. The same is true of the interpretation of a narrative text when all I want to learn is what it narrates—as, for instance, in the interpretation of chronicles or even of Herodotus or Thucydides, when I want to know nothing more than the historical relations and processes that they recount. The same holds good even of a Hellenistic novel, which narrates fictitious happenings but which I read as an entertaining story. In the one case, the objective of understanding is historical instruction, in the other, entertainment. But in both cases the way of asking questions is quite naive, as becomes clear when the text to be understood is a poetic text of distinction such as Homer, which, however, is not read as poetry but, as is often the case to begin with, simply as narration, very much in the way in which works of graphic and plastic art are viewed by naive observers, especially children, by asking what they are about. In part, of course, the fine arts themselves have just such a meaning as illustration, as in "illuminated" manuscripts of the Bible or in cycles of mosaics such as those in the cathedral of Monreale. It is in principle the same kind of thing when in the modern world a Goethe album is published with illustrations of Goethe's life.

But the whole business soon becomes more complicated, for a naive way of questioning the text does not last beyond the stage of childhood even if it never ceases to be justified as a way of asking about what the text directly intends to communicate. The naive way of questioning retains its place especially in the case of scientific texts that seek to mediate knowledge directly. Even when the questioning proceeds to the point of understanding the texts as sources for the history of the science concerned, there is no excluding a prior understanding of what they directly transmit by way of knowledge. Thus, even an interest in the history of mathematics normally remains oriented to mathematical knowledge itself, and thus to the subject matter intended by the texts in question, as distinct from subordinating its interpretation to some other interest, say, in the history of culture. This is illustrated, for example, by the fact that the historian of culture, from the other side, can ignore the history of mathematics, as Jacob Burckhardt actually does in his *Kultur der Renaissance*. Even so, the objective has become different when scientific texts are read simply as so many witnesses for the history of science.

A similar modification occurs in a twofold way in the interpretation of narrative, particularly historical, texts. In the first place, they are not read primarily as witnesses to what they report but rather as witnesses to their own time, out of which they do their reporting. This can still be done in keeping with the intention of the reporter insofar as historical knowledge of the reporter provides a critical standard for understanding his or her report. But in the second place, historical texts can be interpreted as witnesses to the history of historiography, or of the science of history. In this case the intention of the text is completely disregarded, for it does not intend to communicate the science of history but intends, rather, to recount history itself. Nevertheless, it is now put in its own place in history and no longer interpreted as the mediator of historical knowledge but rather as the object thereof.

What about a novel? Even the naive reader does not read merely with a curious interest in what is happening; in straining to learn what is yet to happen, the reader is moved by more than curiosity, namely, by inner participation in the fate of the hero with whom the reader has identified. The reader not only comes to know something but rather shares in the experience of something, being "gripped," with his or her affections touched and passions aroused. And is it not this that alone fulfills the author's intention?

This way of understanding is indeed appropriate in the case of genuine works of literature. They disclose themselves to participatory understanding, as Aristotle in his way already pointed out by his teaching that pity and terror are the effect of tragedy. And what they disclose to such participatory understanding is human existence and its possibilities as also the possibilities of anyone who understands them.

Of such a kind, however, is not only the appropriate understanding of literature and of the effect that it makes possible but the appropriate understanding of art in general. If one may describe the beautiful as "the true expressed in what is visible,"[17] and if one understands "the true" in a radical sense as the disclosure of human existence, which is disclosed by art as the power of displaying the true in the beautiful, then interpretation should understand the possibilities of human existence that are expressed in art as well as in literature.

"The true" is made visible in literature and in art, and it is to be appropriated there by participatory understanding. But it is also the object of reflective and investigative thinking insofar as it becomes the object of philosophy. Therefore, if the interpretation of philosophical texts is really to be understanding, it itself has to be motivated by the question of truth, that is, it can take place only as a discussion with the author. One understands Plato only if one philosophizes with him. Interpretation fails of real understanding when it questions the statements of the text as so many results of research, and when, as a consequence, it takes a particular text as a "source" for a certain stage in the history of philosophy, viewing this history as a happening in the past instead of raising it to the level of the present. There is indeed no need to abandon real philosophical understanding in order to describe the history of philosophy. But this description must be done in such a way that understanding philosophy's history becomes an understanding of philosophy itself, in that through this history the problem of understanding being and therewith of understanding oneself becomes clear.

V

The right way of asking questions in interpreting the texts and monuments of literature and art, philosophy and religion, had to be acquired anew after it had been suppressed by the prevailing way of asking questions during the period of so-called historicism. This is the interest served by Dilthey's efforts and by his recourse to Schleiermacher. Under the hegemony of historicism, texts and monuments had been understood in different ways as "sources," for the most part as sources for reconstructing a picture of some past age or period of time. They were interpreted as witnesses to some historical epoch or as the parts or phases of some historical process, in which case it made no difference in principle how the historical process was understood, whether as political or social history, as intellectual history, or as the history of culture in the broadest sense.

It is not as though texts and monuments cannot also be understood as "sources." There are, in fact, texts whose contents are such that they deserve to be treated only as sources; they are to be distinguished from "classic" texts and monuments even if the boundaries cannot be sharply drawn. If such documents are to be interpreted as sources, however, they must always already be understood in the sense of their own intention—at least provisionally—and they often are so understood in an unreflective, superficial way. If Plato, for example, is to be used as a source for the culture of fifth century Athens, the contents of his work already have to be understood somehow, else he could not serve as a source at all. Nevertheless, to question his work as a document of the history of culture bypasses his own real intention and hardly even catches sight of it in its real scope and depth. The way of asking questions that takes the text to be a source has its proper place in the service of genuine interpretation. For any interpretation necessarily moves in a circle: on the one hand, the individual phenomenon is understandable in terms of its time and place; on the other hand, it itself first makes its time and place understandable. Understanding Plato in terms of his own time stands in service of a genuine interpretation of Plato and belongs to the sphere of the traditional hermeneutical rules previously discussed.

By analogy, other ways of asking questions that were developed during the period of historicism have a legitimate place in the service of genuine understanding. This is true, say, of Heinrich Wölfflin's interpretation of works of art in the context of the history of style or of the countless studies in the history of types and motifs both in literature and in the fine arts. To be sure, all such studies could also obscure the real question of interpretation. And the same is true of formal analysis of works of literature and art undertaken from the aesthetic standpoint: to carry out such analysis is not to achieve real understanding, even though it can be prepared for by such analysis, as, for example, in Karl Reinhardt's book on Sophocles or in Paul Friedländer's work on Plato.[18] How different an interpretation of the same work of art can be, depending on whether it is guided by interest in the form or by interest in the content, becomes clear when one compares the interpretations of Michelangelo's Last Judgment by Jacob Burckhardt and Graf Yorck von Wartenburg, which Karl Löwith has set alongside one another.[19] Erich Auerbach displays complete mastery in his book *Mimesis* in making the formal analysis of works of literature fruitful for the interpretation of their content.[20]

As we have seen, Dilthey takes genuine understanding of literature and art as well as of works in philosophy and religion to be oriented to the question of understanding unique historical existence; and, as has also become clear, all historical documents whatever can be subjected to this way of asking questions. Can this mode of interpretation be understood any more aptly and precisely? It has already been modified by saying that it involves exhibiting the possibilities of human existence that are disclosed in literature and in art as well as in philosophical and religious texts (see above, pp. 77–78). I now want to try to make this somewhat clearer.

In an essay on J. J. Winckelmann's picture of the Greeks, Fritz Blättner has very instructively contrasted the *intentio recta* and the *intentio obliqua* in the reception of religious works of art.[21] The first presupposes the faith of the observer, who sees the divine that he or she believes in presented as something objective in the work of art; thus it does not at all look upon the work as a work of art, and for its purposes an oleograph of the Madonna would perform the same service as a painting by Raphael or a Pietà by Michelangelo. By contrast, the *intentio obliqua* does not ask about the objective meaning of the work of art, and it is indifferent "whether it sees an Apollo or a St. Sebastian, whether what was objectively meant was a Christ or a Moses or a slave"; it asks about the "humanity" or about the "spirit out of which the work of art arose and of which it was a witness."

This change came about with Winckelmann, who "looked behind what is objectively said and meant to the spirit or genius of the creator and of his or her people and perceived it to be the essential thing in the work" (Blättner). So, too, did the great philologists Friedrich Ast and August Boeckh ask about the "spirit" of antiquity as the whole in the light of which the individual work has to be understood.[22] This is the mode of understanding that was developed by J. G. von Herder and came to dominance with romanticism. Naturally, this way of looking at things can also be combined with historicism, even as Winckelmann discovered the epochs of the history of Greek art; because he held the sequence of these epochs to be regular, he could even be regarded as a precursor of Oswald Spengler. During the time of National Socialism, this way of asking questions—qualified, to be sure, by biologism—was reduced to absurdity, although in its basic idea it is also present in the essays in the history of art by Hermann Grimm, whose aim was to write a history of the national artistic imagination.[23]

Naturally, this way of looking at things has a certain justification; and the relativism that belongs to it (which can have its background in a pantheistic faith in the divinity present in everything human) need not become dominant (or conscious). Thus, in the case of Winckelmann, the spirit that he saw acquiring form in Greek art was the exemplary representation of the human spirit as such, on which human beings in every age have to model themselves.

Dilthey's effort, obviously, is to get beyond this ultimately aestheticizing way of looking at things that was typical of romanticism. He remains caught in it, to be sure, when he takes "sympathy with other psychical states" to be grounded in the happiness to which it gives rise and speaks of the "enchantment" that one "enjoys" when one looks beyond the limits of one's own time to the cultures of the past. Nevertheless, one not only enjoys the enchantment but "also takes the strength of the past into oneself." Because through understanding we "find the history of the soul in all history," we thereby "complete" our own individuality and learn "to come to ourselves understandingly."[24] Sentences such as these make clear that genuine understanding does not have to do with happily viewing other individuality as such but is basically directed to the possibilities of human existence that manifest themselves therein, possibilities that are also possibilities for anyone who understands and that are brought to consciousness precisely through understanding. Thus, genuine understanding is a matter of hearing the question raised in the work or the claim encountered in it, and the "completion" of one's own individuality consists in the richer and deeper disclosure of one's own possibilities, in being called beyond oneself by the work (that is, one's incomplete, inertial self, which is constantly in danger of simply continuing as it is).[25]

Yorck sees more clearly even than Dilthey when he says, in defining himself over against Ranke's writing of history, "If anywhere, it is in history that heaven and earth are one." Lying behind this statement is the view that understanding history does not consist in regarding it aesthetically but is a religious process because the reality of history is not even visible to the spectator who is personally uninvolved. "Ranke is a great eyepiece for which what has disappeared cannot become a reality."[26] Yorck's words make clear how historical understanding is hearing the claim of history and critically reflecting on oneself: "Michelangelo preached the renaissance of morality with the most forceful one-sidedness in the Sistine Chapel. The mute, simple crosses scratched by Christians in the stones of the Mamertine prison came to expression through Luther. If anything is more forceful than Michelangelo's Last Judgment, it is those crosses, points of light in a subterranean heaven, signs of the transcendence of consciousness."[27]

The problem of understanding has been decisively clarified by Martin Heidegger's demonstration that understanding is an "existential," by his analysis of interpretation as the development of understanding, and, above all, by his analysis of the problem of history and his interpretation of the historicity of human existence.[28] Following Heidegger's ideas, Fritz Kaufmann has provided a critical survey of contemporary philosophy of history, from which the meaning of interpreting historical documents understandingly clearly emerges.[29]

VI

Let us now summarize the preceding discussion.

The presupposition of any understanding interpretation is a prior life relation to the subject matter that is directly or indirectly expressed in the text and that provides the objective in questioning it. Without such a life relation in which text and interpreter are bound together, questioning the text and understanding it are impossible, and questioning it is not even motivated. This is also to say that any interpretation is necessarily sustained by a certain preunderstanding of the subject matter that is expressed or asked about.

It is out of interest in the subject matter that there emerges some way of asking questions, some objective in questioning the text, some particular hermeneutical principle. The objective of questioning can be identical with the intention of the text, in which case the text mediates the subject matter asked about directly. But the objective can also grow out of interest in matters that appear in any possible phenomena of human life and, accordingly, in any possible text. In this case, the objective of questioning does not coincide with the intention of the text, and the text mediates the subject matter asked about indirectly.

Thus, for example, the objective of interpretation can be given by an interest in reconstructing the continuum of past history—whether political history, the history of the forms and problems of social life, intellectual history, or the history of culture in the broadest sense. In this case the interpretation will always be determined by the understanding that the interpreter has of history in general.

The objective of interpretation can also be given by a psychological interest, which subjects the texts to some way of asking about psychology, whether individual, social, or religious—for instance, by asking about the psychology of literature or of technology, and so on. In all such cases the interpretation is guided by some presupposed preunderstanding of psychological phenomena.

Or again the objective can be given by an aesthetic interest which subjects the text to a formal analysis and questions a work of art about its structure, its "outer" and "inner" form. This aesthetic interest may be combined with a romantic-religious interest, or it may remain simply in the sphere of stylistic analysis.

Finally, the objective of interpretation can be given by an interest in history as the sphere of life in which human existence takes place, in which we acquire and develop our possibilities, and in which, by reflecting on these possibilities, we each come to an understanding of ourselves and of our own possibilities. In other words, the objective can be given by the question about human existence as one's own existence. The texts that most nearly lend themselves to such questioning are the texts of philosophy and religion and literature. But in principle all texts (like history in general) can be subjected to it. Such questioning is always guided by some prior understanding, some particular understanding of human existence, which can be quite naive, but out of which the categories first emerge that alone make the questioning possible—as when one asks, for example, about "salvation," or about the "meaning" of one's personal life or of history, or about the norms of moral action and of order in human community, and the like. Without such a preunderstanding and the questions guided by it, the texts are dumb. The point, then, is not to eliminate the preunderstanding but to risk it, to raise it to the level of consciousness, and to test it critically in understanding the text. In short, in questioning the text one must allow oneself to be questioned by the text and to give heed to its claim.

With this insight we also find the answer to the skeptical question whether we can achieve objectivity in interpretation and in the knowledge of historical phenomena. If the concept of objective knowledge is taken over from natural science (where, by the way, its traditional meaning has also become problematic today), it is not valid for the understanding of historical phenomena, which are of a different kind from the phenomena of nature. As historical phenomena they do not exist at all without a historical subject who understands them. For facts of the past become historical phenomena only when they become meaningful for a subject who exists in history and participates in it. They become historical phenomena only when they speak, and this they do only for the subject who understands them. This is not to say, of course, that the subject simply attaches a meaning to them by arbitrary preference; it is to say, rather, that they acquire a meaning for anyone who is bound together with them in historical life. Thus, in a certain sense, it belongs to a historical phenomenon that it should have its own future in which it alone shows itself for what it is.

It would be misleading to express this by saying that every historical phenomenon is ambiguous. For even if it is indeed vulnerable to arbitrary interpretation according to preference, it is nevertheless in principle unambiguous for scientific understanding. On the other hand, every historical phenomenon is complex and many-sided; it is open to different ways of asking questions, whether the way of intellectual history, psychology, sociology, or what have you, provided only that it arise out of the historical bond between the interpreter and the phenomenon. Any such way of asking questions leads to objective, unambiguous understanding if the interpretation is carried through in a methodical way. And, naturally, there is no reason to object that real understanding is developed only by discussion and the conflict of opinions; the simple fact that every interpreter is limited in his or her subjective capacity is in principle irrelevant.

Knowledge acquired in a methodical way is "objective," which can only mean "appropriate to the object once it comes within a certain way of asking questions." To call the way of asking questions as such "subjective" is pointless. It may indeed be so called if one considers that it naturally has to be chosen in each case by some subject. But what does "choosing" mean here?[30] The way of asking questions as such does not grow out of individual preference but out of history itself, in which every phenomenon, in keeping with its complex nature, offers different aspects, that is, acquires—or, better, claims—significance in different directions. And it is in this same history that every interpreter, in keeping with the motives present in the variety of historical life, acquires the way of asking questions within which the phenomenon begins to speak.

Thus, the demand that the interpreter has to silence his or her subjectivity and quench any individuality in order to achieve objective knowledge could not be more absurd. It makes sense and is justified only insofar as it means that the interpreter must silence his or her personal wishes with respect to the results of interpretation—such as a wish, say, that the text should confirm a certain (dogmatic) opinion or provide useful guidelines for praxis. Often enough, such wishes have been present in exegesis past and present; and, of course, being without presuppositions with respect to results is as unalterably required in the case of interpretation as in any other scientific research. For the rest, however, this demand completely misjudges the nature of genuine understanding, which presupposes the utmost liveliness of the understanding subject and the richest possible unfolding of his or her individuality. Just as we can succeed in interpreting a work of art or literature only by allowing it to grip us, so we can understand a political or sociological text only insofar as we ourselves are concerned with the problems of political and social life. The same holds good, finally, of the kind of understanding to which Schleiermacher and Dilthey orient their hermeneutical theory and which can be said to be understanding of historical phenomena in the ultimate and highest sense, namely, the interpretation that questions texts about the possibilities of human existence as one's own. Here the "most subjective" interpretation is the "most objective," because the only person who is able to hear the claim of the text is the person who is moved by the question of his or her own existence. The monuments of history "speak to us out of the depth of reality that has produced them only when we ourselves, out of our own readiness for experience, are aware of the problem, the finally insurmountable need and threat, that constitute the ground and the abyss of our being-in-the-world."[31]

VII

Interpretation of the biblical writings is not subject to different conditions of understanding from those applying to any other literature. Beyond question, it is subject first of all to the old hermeneutical rules of grammatical interpretation, formal analysis, and explanation in terms of contemporary conditions. But then it is clear that here, also, the presupposition of understanding is the bond between the text and the interpreter, which is established by the interpreter's prior relation to the subject matter mediated by the text. Here, too, the presupposition of understanding is a preunderstanding of the subject matter.

This assertion is contested today by the claim that the subject matter of holy scripture, especially of the New Testament, is the act of God. Of this act there simply cannot be any preunderstanding because we human beings do not naturally have any prior relation to God but rather can know of God only through God's revelation, and thus through God's act.

This counterclaim is only apparently right. It is indeed true that one can no more have a preunderstanding of God's act as a real event than one can have of other events as events. Before I learn from tradition about the death of Socrates I can know nothing about it, anymore than I can know about the assassination of Julius Caesar or Martin Luther's posting of his Ninety-Five Theses. But in order to understand these events as historical events and not merely as arbitrary happenings, I have to have a preunderstanding of the historical possibilities within which they acquire their significance and therewith their character as historical events. I have to know what it means to lead a life of philosophical inquiry, what makes happenings into political events, or what Catholic and Protestant self-understandings are as possibilities open to human beings who must decide who they are to be. (It is hardly necessary to observe that such knowledge naturally need not be explicit.)

Likewise, understanding reports of events as the act of God presupposes a preunderstanding of what in general can be called God's act—as distinct, say, from the acts of human beings or from natural events. And if it is objected that we human beings cannot know who God is and hence also cannot know what God's act means prior to God's revelation, the proper reply is that we can very well know who God is in the question about God. Unless our existence were moved (consciously or unconsciously) by the question about God in the sense of Augustine's "Thou hast made us for thyself, and our heart is restless until it rests in thee," we would not be able to recognize God as God in any revelation. There is an existential knowledge of God present and alive in human existence in the question about "happiness" or "salvation" or about the meaning of the world and of history, insofar as this is the question about the authenticity of our own existence. If the right to describe this question as the question about God is first acquired by faith in God's revelation, still the phenomenon as such is a relation to the subject matter of revelation.

This existential knowledge of God is always somehow interpreted wherever it is consciously present. If it becomes conscious, for example, in the question, "What must I do to be saved?" (Acts 16:30), some idea of "salvation" is necessarily presupposed. Any question directed to the New Testament must be prepared to have the idea that it brings with it corrected by hearing the word of the New Testament itself, and yet it can receive such correction only if the basic intention of the question interpreted by the concept of "salvation" concurs with the intention of the answer given in the New Testament.

So far at least as the scientific exegesis of theology is concerned, everything turns on the appropriate interpretation of the question, and this means at the same time the appropriate interpretation of what it means to be a human being. To work this out is a matter of human reflection, and concretely it is the task of a philosophical, existentialist analysis of human existence. Of course, this kind of work is not a presupposition of a simple hearing of the word of the

New Testament, which is addressed directly to existential self-under-standing and not to existentialist knowledge. But it is otherwise in the case of a scientific interpretation of scripture. It finds its objective by asking about the understanding of human existence that scripture brings to expression. Consequently, it has to concern itself with the appropriate concepts for talking about human existence.

These are grounded in the exegete's life relation to the subject matter expressed in scripture and include a preunderstanding of it. It is an illusion to think that one can do without such a preunder-standing, and the concepts flowing from it, and understand a single word of the New Testament as word of God. The interpreter is in need of critical reflection on the appropriate concepts precisely when he or she seeks to let scripture itself speak to the present as a power addressing our own existence, and thus does not treat the biblical writings as a compendium of dogmatic statements, or as "sources" for reconstructing a bit of past history, or for studying some particular religious phenomenon or the essence of religion in general, or for learning about the psychological development and objectification of religious experiences. If the objective of interpretation is said to be the question about God, or about God's revelation, this means that it is the question about the truth of human existence. But then interpreta-tion has to concern itself with the conceptuality of an existentialist understanding of existence.

VIII

Karl Barth rejects the opinion that a theological statement can be valid only if it can be shown to be a genuine element in the Christian understanding of human existence.[32] This is relevant to the present discussion only insofar as theological statements are interpretations of the assertions of scripture, and thus only insofar as Barth disputes my existentialist interpretation of scripture. This he does in the fol-lowing passage (which in context has to do with the chief statements of the Christian confession): "They [sc. these statements] are indeed all related to human existence. They ground and make possible a Christian understanding of it, and so—inflected—also become deter-minations of human existence. But this is not what they are to begin with. To begin with, they determine the being and action of the God who is other than us human beings and who encounters us: Father, Son, and Holy Spirit. For this reason they are not to be reduced to statements about the inner life of a human being."

The last sentence betrays a complete misunderstanding of existentialist interpretation and of what it means by human existence. This is in no way "the inner life of a human being," which can be understood apart from all that is other than it and encounters it (whether the environment, fellow human beings, or God). This may indeed be how psychology of religion, say, considers human existence, but it is not the way of existentialist analysis. For such analysis seeks to grasp and understand the actual (historical) existence of human beings, who exist only in a context of life with "others," and thus in encounters. Existentialist analysis endeavors to develop an appropriate conceptuality for just such an understanding. But Barth evidently orients his notion of it to a concept of anthropology derived from Ludwig Feuerbach, which he even attributes to Wilhelm Herrmann, instead of seeing that Herrmann was struggling to understand human existence as historical (even if in an inadequate conceptuality).

The demand to make of Barth is that he give an account of his own conceptuality. He grants my claim, for example, that the resurrection of Jesus is not a historical fact that could be established as such by means of the science of history. But it does not follow from this, he thinks, that the resurrection did not occur: "Is it not possible for a story to have really happened and for an acknowledgement of the story to be legitimate even in a case where, simply for reasons of good taste, one would not speak of 'historical fact' and where the 'historian' may very well prefer to speak of 'saga' or 'legend' because the story does indeed elude the means and methods, together with the tacit presuppositions, of this historian?"[33]

I ask, What does Barth understand here by "story" and "happened"? What kind of an event is it of which one can say that "it far more certainly really happened in time than all the things that the historians as such can establish"?[34] It is perfectly clear that Barth interprets the statements of scripture by means of a conceptuality that he brings with him. But what is the source and meaning of this conceptuality?

Furthermore, what way of "believing" is it if credence is to be given to the assertion of events that are supposed to have happened in time and history and yet cannot be established by the means and methods of historical science? How do such events come within the purview of the believer? And how is such faith to be distinguished from a blind acceptance by means of a *sacrificium intellectus*? In what sense does Barth appeal to a demand for honesty that is of another or higher kind than the demand for honesty that requires me to hold nothing to be true that contradicts the truths which are the factual presuppositions of the understanding of the world that guides everything I do?[35] What elements are contained in the mythical world picture to which we do not have to commit ourselves as a whole, but from which we can appropriate certain things eclectically?[36] To ask about a valid meaning of the mythical world picture is precisely the intention of my existentialist interpretation of myth, in which I attempt to proceed methodically, even while all I can find in Barth are arbitrary assertions. What is *his* principle of selection?

It is clearly in Barth's sense that Walter Klaas confronts me with the statement: "One interprets scripture who allows it alone to be the rule and guide of proclamation [where do I dispute this?], who knows the word of prophets and apostles to be foreordained and repeats it as one has responsibly heard it."[37] Such a statement shows only that the person making it still does not see the problem of interpreting scripture. The exegete is supposed to "interpret" scripture after he or she has responsibly "heard" its word. But how is one to hear without understanding? The problem of interpretation is precisely the problem of understanding.

NOTES

1. W. Dilthey, *Die Entstehung der Hermeneutik* (1900), published with additions from the manuscripts in the *Gesammelte Schriften*, 5 (1924), 317–83. The passages quoted above are from pp. 332–33 and 317.

2. Ibid., 317, 334.

3. Ibid., 319.

4. The presentation of hermeneutics in the substantial article by G. Heinrici in the *Realenzyklopädie für protestantische Theologie und Kirche*, 7 (1899), 718–50, is limited to the development of the traditional hermeneutical rules. The same is true of F. Torm's *Hermeneutik des Neuen Testaments* (1930), while E. Fascher, in *Vom Verstehen des Neuen Testaments* (1930), seeks to go further without, in my opinion, ever finding a clear direction. Joachim Wach portrays the "basic features of a history of hermeneutical theory in the nineteenth

century" in his great work, *Das Verstehen*, 3 vols. (1926, 1929, 1933), which is an extraordinarily careful inventory, but in my judgment is far too reserved in taking a position that could have critically illumined the history. The hermeneutical principles that Wach sketches in the *Journal of Biblical Literature* 55 (1936): 59–63 are also merely the old hermeneutical rules, augmented only by the "necessity of psychological understanding," by which he evidently intends to validate Schleiermacher's demand, but without further developing it by consistently working out Dilthey's suggestions. Also, his article on "understanding" in *Religion in Geschichte und Gegenwart*, 5 (2d ed., 1931), 1570–73 is—understandably enough—too sketchy. Fritz Buri engages the discussion of the problem of hermeneutics in contemporary Protestant theology in a critical way in *Schweizerische theologische Umschau, Festgabe für Martin Werner zum 60. Geburtstag* (1947). I find myself close to him both in his struggle for a historical-critical understanding of scripture and in his rejection of a "pneumatic-superhistorical understanding of scripture" and a so-called theological hermeneutics by means of which one practices a "christological exegesis" of the Old Testament. That he has not correctly understood my own efforts is certainly due in part to my not having previously distinguished clearly between a scientific understanding of scripture and obedience to the kerygma. But it is due, above all, to his not having grasped the distinction between existentialist and existential understanding, as becomes clear when he speaks of my attempt at an "existential exegesis," against which I can only protest. He cites my statement from *Offenbarung und Heilsgeschehen* (1941), 41 [in this volume, pp. 14–15] that there should be an "existentialist" interpretation of New Testament mythology by writing "existential" in place of "existentialist."

5. See Dilthey, *Gesammelte Schriften*, 5 (1924), 321, and for what follows, 321ff.

6. H. Patzer, "Der Humanismus als Methodenproblem der klassischen Philologie," *Studium Generale* 1 (1948), 84–92.

7. Aside from Dilthey, see especially Wach, *Das Verstehen*, 1 (1926), 83ff., 102ff., 143, 148–49.

8. The formulations follow Dilthey's characterization in *Gesammelte Schriften*, 5 (1924), 327–28; see also 328, 335.

9. Ibid., 329. See Wach, *Das Verstehen*, 1 (1926), 141. Schleiermacher grounded the process of divinatory understanding in the fact that, while each human being is unique, he or she also has a "receptiveness" for all others.

10. Dilthey, *Gesammelte Schriften*, 5 (1924), 329–30, 334, 332.

11. Ibid., 326–27.

12. G. Misch, *Geschichte der Autobiographie*, 1 (1907).

13. The formula according to which the real goal of exegesis is understanding the author and his or her work (H. Gunkel, *Monatsschrift für die kirchliche Praxis* [1904]: 522), is correct insofar as it denies that exegesis should (or may) be guided by dogmatic or practical interests. But for the rest, it says

nothing whatever about the hermeneutical problem, which begins at this very point. For what understanding of the author is meant? A psychological one? A biographical one? etc. And how is the work to be understood? As belonging to the history of some problem? Aesthetically? etc.

14. This insight is obviously intended in the "idealistic metaphysics of understanding, according to which historical understanding is possible only on the basis of an identity of the human spirit in its diverse objectifications and of this spirit with the absolute Spirit" (Buri, *Schweizerische theologische Umschau* [1947]: 25). But even J. C. K. von Hofmann sees in his way what is decisive here when he says that biblical hermeneutics does not pretend to be an independent science closed in upon itself but rather presupposes general hermeneutics, even though in doing so it does not consist simply in applying general hermeneutics to the Bible but presupposes a relation to the Bible's contents (*Biblische Hermeneutik* [1880], 1ff.). On Hofmann, see also Wach, *Das Verstehen*, 2 (1929), 365, 369–70.

15. This is the sense in which the "congeniality" demanded of the historian by Wilhelm von Humboldt, August Boeckh, and especially Johann Gustav Droysen is also understood. On this, see H. Astholz, *Das Problem "Geschichte" untersucht bei Johann Gustav Droysen* (1933); she cites, among other things, Droysen's characteristic statement that "every human being is indeed a historian, but whoever makes ἱστορεῖν his or her vocation has something to do that is in a special degree human" (97–98).

16. N. Söderblom, *Das Werden des Gottesglaubens* (1916), 41ff.

17. Patzer, *Studium Generale* 1 (1948): 90.

18. K. Reinhardt, *Sophokles* (2d ed., 1943); P. Friedländer, *Platon*, 2: *Die platonischen Schriften* (1930). I may also refer to Reinhardt's lectures and essays, which appeared under the title *Von Werken und Formen* (1948).

19. *Theologische Rundschau*, N.F. 2 (1930): 44–46.

20. E. Auerbach, *Mimesis, Dargestellte Wirklichkeit in der abendländischen Literatur* (1946). In his *Bildnisstudien* (1947), E. Buschor attempts to make stylistic analysis serviceable for what one may well call an existentialist interpretation, even if its categories are insufficiently clear.

21. F. Blättner, "Das Griechenbild J. J. Winckelmanns," *Jahrbuch "Antike und Abendland"* 1 (1944): 121–32.

22. See Wach, *Das Verstehen*, 1 (1926), 106, 185.

23. See R. Buchwald's Foreword to the essays of Hermann Grimm that have appeared under the title *Deutsche Künstler*.

24. The formulations follow Dilthey, *Gesammelte Schriften*, 5 (1924), 317, 328, and the survey by F. Kaufmann, "Geschichtsphilosophie der Gegenwart," *Philosophische Forschungsberichte* 10 (1931): 109–17.

25. See Kaufmann, *Philosophische Forschungsberichte* 10 (1931): 54–55 for a discussion with Simmel about being personally related to the occurrence of history. On hearing the claim of history in Droysen, see Astholz, *Das Problem*

"Geschichte" undersucht bei J. G. Droysen (1933), 106, and 120-21 on understanding as a concern of life and as an act.

26. *Briefwechsel zwischen Wilhelm Dilthey und dem Grafen Paul Yorck von Wartenburg 1877-1897* (1923), 60.

27. Ibid., 120.

28. M. Heidegger, *Sein und Zeit*, 1 (1927), especially paragraphs 31 and 32. Concerning Heidegger, see Kaufmann, *Philosophische Forschungsberichte* 10 (1931):118ff.

29. See Kaufmann, *Philosophische Forschungsberichte* 10 (1931): 41: Understanding a historical context of life is understanding "how human existence once understood or misunderstood its own problem, either standing up to it or fleeing from it." See also Droysen in Astholz, *Das Problem "Geschichte" untersucht bei J. G. Droysen* (1933), 121.

30. Insofar as it is not the forced and accidental choice of a theme for a dissertation.

31. Kaufmann, *Philosophische Forschungsberichte* 10 (1931): 41.

32. K. Barth, *Die kirchliche Dogmatik*, 3/2 (1948), 534.

33. Ibid., 535.

34. Ibid., 535-36.

35. Ibid., 536.

36. Ibid., 536-37.

37. Walter Klaas, *Der moderne Mensch in der Theologie Rudolf Bultmanns* (1947), 29. This writing is a pertinent and sympathetic contribution to the discussion. It is to be regretted only that the author clearly has not understood the meaning of "demythologizing" as a hermeneutical principle and does not know to distinguish between existential and existentialist understanding

ON THE PROBLEM
OF DEMYTHOLOGIZING

(1952)

It is impossible to go into all of the critical comments and to respond to all of the questions addressed to me since the first appearance of my essay, "New Testament and Mythology."[1] But I will try to clarify the questions that seem to me to be the most important.[2]

I. THE POINT OF MYTH
AND OF DEMYTHOLOGIZING

I do not reckon the question about the concept of "myth" among the most important. On the contrary, it seems to me that discussion of this question leads away from what is really at stake in the problem of demythologizing. Anyone who takes my concept of myth to be questionable and wants to understand something else by it is free to do so. I understand by "myth" a very specific historical phenomenon and by "mythology" a very specific mode of thinking. What is at issue is this phenomenon and this mode of thinking.

I use the concept "myth" in the sense in which it is customarily used in the science of history and of religion.[3] Myth is the report of an occurrence or an event in which supernatural, superhuman forces or persons are at work (which explains why it is often defined simply as history of the gods). Mythical thinking is the opposite of scientific thinking. It refers certain phenomena and events to supernatural, "divine" powers, whether these are thought of dynamistically or animistically or are represented as personal spirits or gods. It thus separates off certain phenomena and events as well as certain

95

domains from the things and occurrences of the world that are familiar and that can be grasped and controlled. Scientific thinking, by contrast, is preformed in the "work thinking" that also reckons with a closed continuum of cause and effect; in fact, scientific thinking is basically the radical development of such work thinking and presupposes both the unity of the world and the lawfully regulated order of things and occurrences in the world.[4] As authentically scientific thinking it arises with the question about the ἀρχή, in the sense of the unity-giving cause or source of the world's multiplicity. And by the very fact that this source is now no longer sought, as in mythical thinking, in an otherworldly power or deity, which is represented as preceding the world in time, but rather is thought of as a cause that is immanent in the world and ever present, the difference between mythical and scientific thinking becomes clear. Correlative with the unity of the world in scientific thinking is the unity of scientific thinking itself, which is determined by the λόγον διδόναι, by the justification that must be given for every statement, in contrast to the lack of connection typical of mythical narratives. If Hesiod provides such connection for the old myths, this only shows how myth was reworked by the scientific thinking of the Greeks.

For mythical thinking the world and occurrences in the world are "open"—namely, to the intervention of otherworldly powers—and, therefore, from the viewpoint of scientific thinking are full of gaps. For scientific thinking, by contrast, the world and its occurrences are "closed"—namely, against the intervention of nonworldly powers— although even for science they are also "open," insofar as knowledge of the world and of its occurrences is always incomplete and inconclusive. The world is understood to be closed in the sense of the Aristotelian συνεχές, of that which is continuous, even though knowledge of the unity of the cosmos and of its lawful order never comes to an end.

It is also quite beside the point to observe that the world picture of natural science today is no longer that of the nineteenth century; and it is naive to try to exploit the fact that the law of causality has now been relativized with respect to atomic processes in order to repristinate a mythical faith in wonders—as though such relativizing had opened the door to the intervention of transcendent powers! Has natural science today given up experimentation? As long as it has not

it stands in the tradition of thinking that begins in ancient Greece
with the question about the ἀρχή and the demand for the λόγον
διδόναι. And anyone who stands in this tradition also knows that all
of the results of science are relative and that any world picture
worked out either yesterday, today, or tomorrow can never be definitive. The decisive thing, however, is not the results of scientific thinking but its method.[5]

For mythical thinking not only the world that science understands
as nature is "open" to the intervention of transcendent powers but
also our personal life as human beings. Those of us who have out-
grown mythical thinking understand our existence as a unity and
attribute our feeling, thinking, and willing to ourselves; we no longer
refer them, as myth does, to the intervention of divine or demonic
powers. This is true whether we are consistent naturalists who understand our personal life merely as a phenomenon of nature, and thus
as dependent on natural processes, or whether we recognize the
independence of our spiritual life over against nature. In the second
case, however, we know about our own freedom and responsibility
for ourselves.[6] The notion typical of mythical thinking that there is a
magical force that can be exercised on our feeling, thinking, and
willing, as well as the notion that our spiritual life can be nourished
by material means, and hence the idea of a sacrament, has now
become alien to us. Even in our relation to God we can understand
ourselves only as personal beings who are addressed by God in our
being as persons. This means that the only speaking and acting of
God that we can understand as important and of concern to us are
such as encounter us in our own personal existence and have to do
precisely with it. We find incredible a theory of satisfaction that
describes God's act as a cultic or juristic act and a Christ occurrence
that cannot be understood as having to do with our own personal
existence.[7]

Myth is frequently called "primitive science." This is correct in the
case of etiological myths, which seek to explain such striking, surpris-
ing, or frightening natural phenomena as eclipses of the sun or moon
or the diverse lengths of the legs of Orion. If we disregard the fact that
etiology appeals to powers that are taken not from observation of
nature but from a specifically mythical understanding of the world,
about which I shall say more presently, then mythical thinking can

indeed be designated as primitive science insofar as it is an inquiring kind of thinking that reckons with cause and effect. This designation is especially apt, however, because myth is an objectifying kind of thinking like that of science. Myth actually talks about transcendent powers or persons as though they were immanent and worldly—contrary to its real intention.

For what is this intention?[8] Myth talks about transcendent powers, about demons and gods as powers on which we know ourselves to be dependent, of which we do not dispose, whose favor we need and whose wrath we fear. It thus makes apparent our knowledge that the world in which we have to live as human beings is full of enigmas and mysteries, that human life itself is also full of enigmas and mysteries, and that we are not lords over the world and our own life. In this way myth gives expression to a certain understanding of human existence. As is documented by the original connection of myth with cult, it knows of another reality than the reality of the world that science has in view. It knows that the world and human life have their ground and limit in a power that lies beyond everything falling within the realm of human reckoning and control—in a transcendent power.

But myth talks about this transcendent reality and power inadequately when it represents the transcendent as spatially distant, as heaven above the earth, or as hell beneath it.[9] It talks about the transcendent powers inadequately when it represents them as analogous to immanent powers and as superior to these powers only in force and unpredictability. This is clear from the mythical concept of wonder, or miracle. For it represents the working of transcendent power (the action of God) as an occurrence that at once breaks through the natural or psychological course of occurrences and links them together. Transcendent causality is inserted into the causal chain of events in the world, and a power that in this sense works a miracle is conceived, for better or worse, as a worldly power and projected onto the plane of worldly occurrences. Myth talks about gods as human beings, and about their actions as human actions, with the difference that the gods are represented as endowed with superhuman power and their actions as unpredictable and able to break through the natural run of things. Myth thus makes the gods (or God) into human beings with superior power, and it does this even when it speaks of God's omnipotence and omniscience, because it does not distinguish these qualitatively from human power and knowledge but only quantitatively.

In short, myth objectifies the transcendent into the immanent, and thus also into the disposable, as becomes evident when cult more and more becomes action calculated to influence the attitude of the deity by averting its wrath and winning its favor.

Demythologizing seeks to bring out the real intention of myth, namely, its intention to talk about human existence as grounded in and limited by a transcendent, unworldly power, which is not visible to objectifying thinking.

Thus, negatively, demythologizing is criticism of the mythical world picture insofar as it conceals the real intention of myth. Positively, demythologizing is existentialist interpretation, in that it seeks to make clear the intention of myth to talk about human existence.[10]

Accordingly, demythologizing of the biblical writings is criticism of the mythological world picture of the Bible, and the objection immediately arises that the modern world picture is thereby made the critical standard for interpreting scripture. In point of fact, scientific thinking does destroy the mythological world picture of the Bible; in the conflict between the objectifying thinking of myth and the objectifying thinking of science the second is naturally the victor. But demythologizing interpretation seeks through its criticism to bring out the real intention of the biblical writings. It sees that we cannot talk about God or what transcends the world as it is "in itself," because in doing so we would objectify God or the transcendent into an immanent, worldly phenomenon. Demythologizing thus seeks to proceed according to Philipp Melanchthon's dictum, "To know Christ is to know his benefits, not to contemplate his natures and the mode of his incarnation," or the dictum of Wilhelm Herrmann, "We cannot say of God how he is in himself but only what he does to us."[11] Such interpretation oriented by the question about our existence is existentialist interpretation. Its criticism of the biblical writings lies not in eliminating mythological statements but in interpreting them; it is not a process of subtraction but a hermeneutical method.

If its point is correctly grasped it seems absurd to concede the appropriateness of demythologizing for certain peripheral statements in the New Testament, only to contest it for the central statements.[12]

As if the problem were not then really urgent! The motive underlying this distinction is clearly anxiety that demythologizing the central statements would lead to abandoning talk about God's act and about a salvation occurrence that takes place in history. But the assumption that such talk must of necessity be mythological talk is to be disputed.

Of course, it is often claimed that the language of faith, like that of religion generally, must necessarily be mythological, because our language is otherwise lacking in concepts in which to talk appropriately about God and God's act.[13] But typically those who assert the indispensability of mythological language nevertheless seek to escape from mythical thinking and understand mythological concepts and representations as—to be sure, indispensable—pictures or "symbols." Obviously, they do not recognize that they themselves are thereby demythologizing and that their own practice refutes their assertion.[14]

Are mythological representations and concepts really indispensable? They may be so in a provisional sense insofar as truths are intended in them that cannot be expressed in the language of objectifying science. In that case mythological language provisionally expresses that for which adequate language must still be found. Thus, the task that is set for thinking (although not for the thinking of objectifying science!) can be formulated in mythological language in the way in which this happens in the Platonic myths.[15] Nevertheless, the usual way of talking about mythical concepts and representations as "pictures" and "symbols" has to be patient of the question about the point of such pictures and symbols. For, clearly, they are supposed to express some point, and is it also to be formulated in mythological language, so that the point of this language must in turn be interpreted—and so on in infinitum? This is evidently absurd, and in fact even representatives of the symbol theory (if one may so speak of them) are given to offering interpretations in nonmythological language.

Who among them still understands the statement that God is the Creator in the sense of myth? Or the statements about God's throne being in heaven and Christ's sitting at God's right hand? What is meant when Helmut Thielicke summons us "to make visible the ground in reality behind the mythical covering"?[16] Is this not to demythologize? And is it not existentialist interpretation when

Thielicke allows as an essential truth that "one cannot stop simply with the representations of the mythical world picture but has to work out their existential reference"? Again, does not Julius Schniewind demythologize when he says that the "mythological" portrayals of the day of judgment are only supposed to direct our attention to the subject matter that is really intended? "The final judgment," he says, "is eschatological in the strictest sense: it takes place beyond our space and our time; it takes place 'in another world,' where each individual as well as humanity as a whole is placed beyond this space of ours and this time of ours."[17] Or is it not demythologizing when Schniewind says that the preexistence of Jesus means "that God himself is present in Jesus' words and deeds"?[18] It is also demythologizing, albeit unclearly, when Thielicke speaks of the virgin birth as "a picture of the historical fact of being the Son of God."[19]

In many cases we demythologize unintentionally and unreflectively by taking the mythological statements of the Bible as pictures that have long since lost their original mythical sense. This is done most easily, naturally, with poetic writings in the Bible like the Psalms, in which the mythological language may in many cases already have been intended poetically. In our daily life, also, we use pictures that stem from mythical thinking, as when we say, for example, that our heart prompts us to do this or that—a statement that no one understands any longer in its original mythological sense. But those of us who have to interpret scripture responsibly ought to be conscious of what we are doing and to remind ourselves that honesty at this point requires us to be radical.

Anxiety about demythologizing may be due in part to the unquestioned assumption that there is an either/or between mythology and science, where by "science" is understood the science that objectifies existence into being within the world. But is there no other language than the language of science and of myth? Are statements like "I love you" or "Pardon me" expressed in the language of science? Or if they are not, is the language in which they are expressed mythological? There is in fact a language in which existence naively expresses itself, and, correspondingly, there is a science that talks about existence without objectifying it into being within the world.

It should be clear that demythologizing in the sense of existentialist interpretation seeks, in critically interpreting the mythical world picture of scripture, to bring out the point of its statements by freeing them from the conceptuality of objectifying thinking—the objectifying thinking of myth. But naturally it does not do this only to leave these statements to the conceptuality of the objectifying thinking of science. On the contrary, demythologizing wants an understanding of scripture that is free of every world picture projected by objectifying thinking, whether it is that of myth or that of science.

The objection that demythologizing wants to make the gospel "scientifically respectable," where by "science" is understood the science of objectifying thinking, is nonsense. The statements of scripture that speak out of existence and to existence do not have to justify themselves before the forum of an objectifying science that cannot even take account of existence. On the contrary, because demythologizing through its criticism of the biblical world picture removes the scandal that this world picture necessarily poses for us as modern men and women, it exposes the real scandal that the Bible presents to us moderns just as to all other human beings. This scandal lies in the fact that God's word calls us out of all our anxiety as well as all our self-contrived security to God, and thereby to our own authentic existence, to freedom from the world that we take possession of by the objectifying thinking of science in such a way that we thereby give it power over us. Faith as the surrender of self-security as well as the overcoming of the despair that arises from striving for such security is at once the demand and the gift of the proclamation; faith is the answer to the question of the kerygma that is addressed precisely to me. This faith that God calls me and acts on me can be laid hold of and maintained only by a "nevertheless" over against the world; for neither God nor God's act can be visible in a world that constantly seeks its own security and therefore deprives all that it encounters of any existential reference by its objectifying way of viewing things. All mythological talk about God can serve only to conceal this "nevertheless." Demythologizing as existentialist interpretation seeks to make clear the character of scripture as personal address and thereby also to clarify the "nevertheless" that essentially belongs to faith.

Undertaking demythologizing, therefore, leads one to ask about the conceptuality in which the intention of biblical statements can be expressed—about a language in which proclamation, like faith, can talk without misunderstanding. There is no proclamation without concepts, and there is no act of faith that is not at the same time an act of thought (to use a favorite formulation of Adolf Schlatter). It goes without saying that neither proclamation nor faith in itself presupposes reflection on its conceptuality. Nevertheless, in a situation in which understanding of scripture has become uncertain and controversial, in which proclamation is misunderstood or not understood at all, and in which reproduction of traditional confessional statements is supposed to be the language of faith, there is need for such reflection, for thought about the appropriate conceptuality for exegesis, proclamation, and confession. To carry out such reflection is the task of theology, specifically, of hermeneutics, and, therefore, a task of science. Are understanding of scripture, proclamation, and faith then dependent on science? In a certain sense they are, indeed, insofar as science is necessary in order to express the subject matter with which they are concerned. This is already the case because it is necessary to translate the biblical texts into particular contemporary vernaculars; for what is translation if not a science? But the art of translation goes beyond the science of language: it is also the art of interpretation; to philology must be added hermeneutics.[20] It would be an illusion not to recognize that to this extent understanding of scripture and proclamation are dependent on a science—and that the same is true even of faith insofar as it, in turn, depends on proclamation. The only question is what kind of a science and where is the source of its conceptuality.

It is clear that it cannot be the kind of objectifying science that objectifies human being into being within the world. Rather, it can only be a science that is nothing other than the clear and methodical development of the understanding of existence that is given with existence itself—just as, correspondingly, objectifying science is nothing but the consistent and methodical development of the "work thinking" by which we take possession of the world.[21] Provided scripture and proclamation speak out of existence and to existence, and provided faith is an existential self-understanding, there is no reason for concern that exegesis, proclamation, and faith should come under the domination of a science that is essentially alien to them. They should, of course, come under the discipline of a science whose thinking and conceptuality have their source in the subject matter itself, namely, in the self-understanding of existence.

It goes without saying that existentialist interpretation does not produce the existential relation of scripture to the reader; it only discloses this relation. It does not justify the truth of scripture but points to this truth and teaches us to understand it. Similarly, existentialist interpretation of scripture does not justify proclamation, although it does provide proclamation with the right conceptuality. Finally, it does not justify faith, but it shows what the ground of faith is, and it can keep faith from misunderstanding itself. If such interpretation itself is grounded in an existential self-understanding, it must have an understanding of scripture therein that precedes the methodical unfolding of its conceptuality—just as a "life relation" to its object is prior to any science. This understanding, then, is prescientific; it does not need to be already a believing understanding but can be present throughout in the form of a question—the existential question of self-understanding.

But if there is such a prescientific understanding of scripture, and if there is such also as a believing understanding, what is science supposed to do? To begin with it has the task of clearly expressing this understanding and abiding by it, and this means constantly leading back to it; for faith is constantly in danger of missing its point—as an existential self-understanding—and confusing itself with the acceptance of general truths or traditional dogmas. But where the prescientific understanding of scripture is no longer present and—as is the case today—is for many persons obstructed, science also has the task of once again exposing the possibility of such an understanding by destroying misunderstanding.

The objection that the biblical proclamation is "rationalized" by demythologizing is weak if demythologizing is understood as existentialist interpretation. Sometimes this objection is clothed in the charge that the mystery of God's act is set aside. But there is a false notion of the mystery of divine action that underlies this charge, namely, the concept of mystery that stems from objectifying thinking. For this kind of thinking, which occupies itself with research directed toward rationally explaining the world, there are many provisional and presumably definitive mysteries—in any case, mysteries that are continually arising anew. But these mysteries are completely irrelevant to existential self-understanding—at least directly—and have nothing to do with the mystery of God's act. It is sadly misleading when such mysteries are set forth in edifying discourses as the mysteries of God; for this can only lead to concealing the real mystery of God.[22] Demythologizing as existentialist interpretation seeks to make clear and understandable the real mystery of God in its authentic incomprehensibility. Understanding is something different from rationally explaining. I can understand what friendship, fidelity, and love are; and precisely when I understand them rightly I know that the friendship, love, and fidelity shown to me always are and remain a mystery to be gratefully received. I do not grasp them at all by rational thinking, neither by logical inference from the attitude of others nor by psychological analysis, nor even by existentialist analysis.[23] Rather, I grasp them only in the existential openness of my person for encounter. In this openness I already understand what friendship, love, and fidelity are, even before they are given to me, because my existence has need of them: I understand them in the question for them. So, too, I can understand what God's grace means; otherwise I could not talk about it at all. But that this grace encounters *me*, that the gracious God is *my* God, is always a mystery precisely in God's revelation. It is not a mystery, however, because God is an irrational being or does something that breaks into the course of the world in an unintelligible way. It is a mystery, rather, because it is inconceivable that God encounters me.　·

II. DEMYTHOLOGIZING
AND PHILOSOPHY OF EXISTENCE

Demythologizing as a hermeneutical method raises the question of the right conceptuality in which interpretation is to be expressed. It thereby points to a science whose business is the methodical development of the understanding of existence that is given with existence itself—in other words, to philosophy of existence. The objection that interpretation thereby comes to be dominated by a science that is essentially alien to it has already been provisionally answered, but it must now be taken up once again in the special formulation that existentialist interpretation makes itself dependent on philosophy.

First of all, we must bear in mind that any interpretation is guided by a certain way of asking questions without which the interpretation is not even possible. Naturally, this way of asking questions does not have to be conscious or explicit, but without it the texts remain dumb. It also goes without saying that the way of asking questions may not prejudice the contents of what is asked about by presupposing certain results of exegesis; on the contrary, it is supposed to open our eyes for the contents of the text.[24]

I may assume, I think, that the appropriate question with respect to the Bible—at least within the church—is the question about human existence, which is a question I am driven to ask by the existential question about my own existence. This is a question that finally motivates questioning and interpreting historical documents generally; for in the last analysis the point of studying history is to become conscious from it of the possibilities for understanding human existence. Of course, there is yet another reason why this is the question with which I especially turn to the Bible. It lies in the fact (which for any merely profane interest is accidental) that the proclamation of the church refers me to scripture as the place where I will hear something decisive about my existence.[25]

That the Bible, like other historical documents, not only *shows* me a possibility for understanding my existence, which I can decide either to accept or to reject, but beyond this becomes a word addressed to me personally, which *gives* me existence—this is a possibility that I cannot presuppose and reckon with as a methodical principle of interpretation. That it is ever actualized is—in traditional terminology—the work of the Holy Spirit.

As for the objection that I cannot have the kind of prior life relation to the revelation of God attested in scripture, which one must have to the subject matter of any text in order to have the right way of asking questions, it, too, cannot be sustained against existentialist interpretation. For the truth is that I have such a prior life relation in the question about God—in the sense of Augustine's classical formulation, "Thou hast made us for thyself, and our heart is restless until it rests in thee." Consciously or unconsciously, human life is moved by the question about God.

If hearing God's word in faith can only be the work of the Holy Spirit effected by understanding decision, understanding of the text can take place only by methodical interpretation, and the conceptuality guiding such interpretation can be acquired only by the kind of profane reflection that is the business of a philosophical analysis of existence.

In this way exegetical work does indeed become dependent on the work of philosophy. But it would be an illusion to suppose that any exegesis could be carried out independently of some profane conceptuality. Every exegete is dependent—usually unreflectively and uncritically—on some conceptuality made available by tradition, and every traditional conceptuality is in one way or another dependent on some philosophy. It is important, however, not to proceed unreflectively and uncritically but to take account of the conceptuality guiding one's interpretation and the source from which it comes.[26] Thus, one may say without anxiety that what is at issue is the question about the "right" philosophy.

One may say this without anxiety because it does not mean that there is a right philosophy in the sense of some definitive philosophical system—such as idealism, say, and specifically Georg Wilhelm Friedrich Hegel's—and that exegesis has to accept the answers of such a philosophy to the existential question about the meaning of my particular existence. The "right" philosophy is simply the kind of philosophical work that undertakes to develop the understanding of existence that is given with existence itself in an appropriate conceptuality. Therefore, it does not ask the question about the meaning of existence as an existential question but rather inquires by way of existentialist analysis what existence means in general, in the knowledge that the existential question can be answered only by existing itself.

There would be reason to object at this point only if the concept of the authenticity of existence developed by philosophy were thought to be a material ideal of existence—in other words, if philosophy were to prescribe to us: *so* should you exist! But philosophy says to us only: you should *exist!* Or if that is already to say too much, philosophy shows us what existing means. It shows us that human being, in contradistinction from all other being, means precisely to exist—to be a being that is given over to itself and has to take responsibility for itself. Philosophy thus shows us that human existence comes to its authenticity only by existing, and therefore is realized only ever anew in the concrete here and now. It does not propose, however, to create an existential understanding of the here and now by existentialist analysis; it does not take this away from us but rather leaves it precisely to us.[27]

It is clear that existentialist analysis is grounded in the existential questioning of existence. Where else but from being moved by the existential question should it know anything about existence? Its work consists precisely in methodically developing the understanding of existence that is given with existence. But just this is the basis for an objection that F. K. Schumann has developed in a penetrating way.[28] This is the objection that with existentialist analysis decision for a certain understanding of existence has already been made.

Schumann is quite right that there can be no "formal analysis of human existence that can be valid apart from every 'existential' attitude, every actual relation of oneself to one's own existence," and that no "existentialist analysis can be carried out in such a way that it could be valid and applicable apart from the understanding of existence from which it has been acquired." But this is to say nothing other than what I have repeatedly stressed myself in saying that existentialist analysis is simply the methodical unfolding of the self-understanding given with existence. If one wants to say that a decision is already made in existentialist analysis, it is the decision to exist. It is made by the fact that the analysis distinguishes human being as existing from the "being available" of worldly phenomena (that can be grasped by objectifying thinking). But this decision does not close one against any concrete possibilities of existential self-understanding but rather opens one precisely for them. This decision is not an act of methodical philosophical thought but rather a decision in which philosophizing itself is grounded. Or, if one wants to call it "philosophical," there is point in doing so if one is willing to understand philosophizing as a movement essentially belonging to human being. Without this decision, which is to say, simply, without the will to be a human being or person who responsibly takes over his or her own being, no one can understand even a word of scripture as a word addressed to existence.

But that it is not possible by philosophical reflection on the basis of this fundamental decision to project a "purely formal" analysis of existence seems to me to be an unjustified prejudice. To what extent one succeeds at the task is, to be sure, another question. But in principle this is as little to the point as the insight that conclusive knowledge is impossible in any science and philosophy. Any analysis that is ever given naturally remains subject to correction, and progress here as well as elsewhere takes place through discussion.

The possibility of discussion in this case is given by the fact that any existential self-understanding lies within the possibilities of human existence, and, therefore, any existentialist analysis based on such a self-understanding can be generally understood. This also explains why there is some point to the task of working out a formal analysis of existence.

Such an analysis naturally functions as a "norm" insofar as some phenomenon of existence, for example, the phenomenon of love—to stay with Schumann's own example—is to be understood in existentialist terms.[29] But it is a misunderstanding to suppose that it is thereby decided "how I have to understand my own particular love." Precisely the opposite is the case: existentialist analysis can only make clear to me that I can understand "my own particular love" only existentially and that this understanding cannot be taken away from me by any existentialist analysis—as a "norm."

Certainly, a pure existentialist analysis includes the judgment "that it is possible to analyze human existence without considering the 'man-God' relationship."[30] But then is an analysis of human existence that would take God into consideration a meaningful possibility, provided the "man-God" relationship can only be an event in the concrete encounter of a human being with God? A pure analysis of existence cannot in any way consider the "man-God" relationship because it abstracts from the concrete encounters in which existence ever again realizes itself. But in doing this it sets these encounters free. If God's revelation becomes actual only in each particular now of existence (as "eschatological" event), and if existentialist analysis points us to our own temporality in which we each have to exist, it thereby discloses a characteristic of existence that faith—but only faith—understands as our relatedness to God. This understanding, however, is not obstructed by a formal analysis of existence but is rather clarified by it. Likewise, faith's understanding of our being moved by the question about ourselves as our being moved by the question about God is not obstructed but clarified by a formal existentialist analysis.

But may one say, as Schumann does, that the judgment that an analysis of existence is (not only) possible (but alone meaningful) without considering God is an existential predecision? I think one may indeed say this, although not in the sense of Schumann, who evidently understands the judgment in such a way that in it a decision is already made for an existence without God. It is an existential decision insofar as the judgment is based in an insight that one can attain only existentially, that the idea of God is not at our disposal to project a theory of existence. But, of course, the judgment may not be said to be a *pre*decision, as though it were made once and for all prior to the analysis; rather, it is constantly present in the analysis. I can also put it this way: the judgment in question is the self-knowledge or confession, realized only existentially, that when I look into myself I do not find God. Just by virtue of this confession the analysis of existence acquires its "neutrality."

III. TALK ABOUT THE ACT OF GOD

Perhaps one may say that behind all of the objections to demythologizing there lurks the fear that its consistent execution would make it impossible to talk about the act of God or that it could allow such talk only as a pictorial way of designating subjective experiences. For is it not mythology to talk about the act of God as an objective occurrence that encounters me?

The first thing to say by way of an answer is that it certainly is the case that if talk about God's act is to be meaningful it is not pictorial or "symbolic" talk but means to speak of an act in a fully real, "objective" sense. If, however, God's act may not be understood as a phenomenon in the world that I can perceive apart from being existentially affected by it, then it can be talked about only in that I myself, as the one affected by it, am also talked about. To talk about God's act means to talk at the same time about my own existence. Because human life is a life in space and time, God's encounter with us can only be an event in the particular here and now. This event of being addressed, questioned, judged, and blessed by God here and now is what is meant by talk about the act of God.

Therefore, talk about God's act is not a pictorial, symbolic way of talking, although it is analogical talk.[31] For in such talk we represent

God's act as analogous to a human act and the community between God and ourselves as analogous to the community between one human being and another.

The point of such talk, however, needs to be clarified further. Mythological thinking represents divine action—be it in nature or in history, in human destiny or in innerpsychical life—as an action that intervenes in the continuum of natural, historical, or psychical life and disrupts it—in short, as a "wonder." In just this way mythological thinking objectifies divine action and projects it onto the plane of worldly occurrences.[32] But a wonder, that is, an act of God, is not visible to an objectifying view nor can it be established as events in the world can be established. The idea that divine action is unworldly or transcendent is preserved only if such action is represented not as something taking place *between* occurrences in the world but as something that takes place *in* them, in such a way that the closed continuum of worldly occurrences that presents itself to an objectifying view is left intact. God's act is hidden from all eyes other than the eyes of faith. The only thing that can be generally seen and established is the "natural" occurrence. In it God's hidden act takes place.

The immediate objection to this is that Christian faith is thereby transformed into pantheistic piety. But whereas pantheism believes in the *direct* identity of worldly occurrences with divine action, faith asserts their *paradoxical* identity, which can be believed in in each case only against appearances. In faith I can understand an event occurring to me as God's gift or judgment, although I can also view it within its natural or historical context. In faith I can also understand a thought or a decision as effected by God without thereby tearing it out of the continuum of its innerworldly motivation.

Christian faith is not a "world view" like pantheism, which is an already given conviction that all occurrences are divinely effected because God is immanent in the world. Christian faith believes that God acts on me, speaks to me, in each particular situation. It believes this because it knows itself to be addressed by the grace encountering me in the word of Jesus Christ, by the grace that opens my eyes to see that God works for good in everything with those who love him (Rom. 8:28). But such faith is not a knowledge possessed once and for all, not a "world view." It can only be an event, and it can remain alive only in that believers ask in each situation what God would say to them here and now. In general, God is just as hidden in nature and history for believers as for everyone else. But insofar as each concrete occurrence is seen in the light of the word of grace spoken to me, faith should and can accept it as God's doing, even if its meaning remains enigmatic. If pantheism can say of any event whatever, quite apart from what it means for me as I encounter it, "This has been wrought by deity," faith can say only, "God is acting in this or that in a hidden way." *What* God is now doing—and it is not directly identical with the occurrence that can be objectively established—I perhaps do not yet know and maybe never will know. But I must ask what God wants to say to me by it, even if it is only—or precisely—that I should be silent and bear it.

Even faith in God as the Creator is not an already given certainty by virtue of which I am in a position to designate every occurrence as divinely wrought. Such faith can be actualized genuinely only when I understand myself existentially here and now as God's creature, which naturally need not come to consciousness as reflective knowledge. Faith in God's omnipotence is not an already given conviction that there is a being who can do all things, but it can be actualized only existentially by subjecting myself to the power of God that subdues me here and now, which, again, need not be raised to the level of explicit consciousness. Statements of faith are not general truths. For example, that the statement, "The earth everywhere is the Lord's," has lost its point as a known dogma and has a point only when it is made in each situation in an existential decision is certainly best known today by one to whom it has become doubtful in the misery of Russian imprisonment.

It becomes clear from all this that the world loses its character as a closed continuum for my existential life, which is realized in decisions in face of encounters. Put differently, in faith the closed continuum presented (or produced) by objectifying thinking is sublated—not of course in the manner of mythological thinking, so that it is thought of as disrupted, but in such a way that it is sublated as a whole when I talk about God's act. Actually, it is already sublated when I talk about myself; for I myself, in my authentic being, am just as little to be seen and established within the world as is the act of God. When I look upon worldly occurrences as a closed continuum, which I have to do in the interest not only of scientific understanding but also of my daily life and work, then, indeed, there is no room for God's act. But the paradox of faith is that it understands an event that can be established in its natural and historical continuum as nevertheless God's act. This "nevertheless" is inseparable from faith.

Such faith alone is genuine faith in wonders.[33] If we suppose that we can talk about wonders as processes that can be objectively established, we go against the idea that God's act is hidden. We subject God's act to an objectifying view and thereby leave faith in wonders—in truth, superstition about wonders—to justified scientific criticism.

If it is right, then, that we can talk about God's act only if we at the same time talk about our own existence, so that God's act cannot be established outside of our own being affected by it, and hence is lacking in the kind of objectivity that can be established by neutral observation (as in an experiment, say) and scientific thinking (precisely as objectifying thinking)—if this is right, the question naturally arises whether this does not deny to God's act all "objectivity" whatever as a reality lying outside of us as subjects. Is not God's act then drawn completely into the sphere of subjectivity? Is not faith then understood merely as "experience"? Is not God present then only in the "innerpsychical" process of experience, whereas faith makes sense only if it is directed to God who is real outside of the believer?

This objection rests on a psychologistic misunderstanding of what is meant by our existential life as human beings.[34] It by no means follows from what has been said—that only the faith affected by God can talk about God, and that when we as believers talk about God's act we are thereby also talking about ourselves—that God is not real outside of believers or their act of faith. This follows only if faith and experience are interpreted psychologistically.[35] But if human being is understood as in a genuine sense historical being, which has its experiences in its encounters with others, two things are clear: on the one hand, the faith that talks of the act of God encountering it cannot defend itself against the charge of being an illusion—for the encounter with God is not objective in the sense of a worldly event; on the other hand, faith as an existential process of encounter not only has no need to refute this charge but also cannot seek to refute it without misunderstanding its own meaning as faith.

What "encounter" means in general can be clarified simply by reflecting on our historical life. The love of another person encounters me and is what it is only as event; it cannot be perceived as love by an objectifying view but only by me myself as the one affected by it.[36] Seen from the outside it is not visible as love in the genuine sense but only as a historical or psychical phenomenon that is subject to various possibilities of interpretation. Naturally, the reality of the love with which another person loves me does not depend on my understanding it and responding with love in return.[37] (This I know precisely when I respond to it with returning love.) Even if I do not understand it or open myself to it, it still calls forth an existential reaction, so to speak; ignoring it is such a reaction, as is closing myself against it or hate. In either case I am qualified by the encounter. And yet this in no way changes the fact that it is visible as love only in the encounter itself.

That God is not visible outside of faith does not mean that God is not real outside of faith. That encounter with God's word qualifies us whether we open ourselves to it or not is also known only by the faith that understands God's judgment to take place in unfaith.

Certainly, faith in its relation to its object is not provable. But as Herrmann already taught us, the fact that faith cannot be proved is precisely its strength.[38] To claim that faith could be proved would imply that God could be known and established outside of faith and thus put God on the same level as the available world that can be disposed of by an objectifying view.[39] Of course, within the world it is appropriate to demand that things be proved.

But if faith is the answer to the proclaimed word of God's grace which has its origin and legitimation in the New Testament, must not one say that it is proved by appeal to scripture? Is it not simply hearing of scripture as the word of God? This is indeed correct, and yet it is so only when scripture is understood neither as a compendium of doctrines nor as a document containing the faith of others, which can bring about certain innerpsychical experiences by means of "empathy." It is correct only when scripture is heard as provocative word, as personal address, as kerygma, and thus when "experience" is a matter of being affected by and responding to the address. That scripture is God's word takes place only here and now in each particular situation; it is not a fact that can be objectively established. God's word is hidden in scripture just as any act of God is hidden.[40]

Nor is God proved by so-called facts of salvation, for these facts themselves are the object of faith and are first visible as such to faith and to it alone. Knowledge of them does not precede faith, so that it could be grounded on such knowledge in the way in which a conviction is otherwise grounded on evident facts. Of course, these facts justify faith, and yet they do so only as perceived in faith itself—just as among ourselves trust and love are not grounded on the trustworthiness and love of the other person as things that can be objectively established but are grounded on the being of the other that is perceived in trust and in love. There is neither trust nor love without risk. Thus—as Herrmann also already taught us—the ground and the object of faith do not fall asunder but are one and the same; and this is so precisely because we cannot say of God how he is in himself but only what he does to us.[41]

If, then, the act of God is not visible within the world and cannot be proved, if the "salvation occurrence" is not a process that can be objectively established, if—as we may add—the Spirit given to faith is not a phenomenon that can be perceived within the world, if we can talk about all of these things only in that we talk about our own existence, then it may also be said that faith is a new understanding of existence or that God's act gives us a new self-understanding, in keeping with Martin Luther's statement, "And so, in going out of himself, God brings it about that we go into ourselves; and through knowledge of him he brings us to knowledge of ourselves."[42]

And yet it is against this designation of faith as an understanding of existence that the attacks against demythologizing have above all been directed.[43] Is it really so hard to understand what is meant by "existential self-understanding"? In any case, there is nothing but complete lack of understanding behind the objection that by this designation the event of revelation is degraded to the occasion that releases self-understanding and therefore is no longer acknowledged as a fact that intervenes in reality and transforms it, and thus as a wonder. According to this objection, the only thing that happens is "consciousness." The content of self-understanding is a timeless truth, which, once it becomes known, remains valid without reference to the occasion that released it or, so to say, "cranked it up."[44] Did Luther understand "knowledge of ourselves" to mean this?

But perhaps because of unclear formulations I myself am partly to blame for the confusion that lies at the bottom of this misunderstanding. In any case, existential understanding is here confused with the existentialist understanding of human being that philosophical analysis works out. Of the second one can certainly say that statements expressing it have the meaning of timeless truths and, insofar as they are to the point, can be valid as such. But existentialist analysis points beyond itself, so to speak, in that it shows (and this, too, would be a "timeless truth") that existential self-understanding takes place only as my own particular self-understanding in existential decision. In my existential self-understanding I do not understand in general what existence is (that would be existentialist understanding), but I understand myself in my concrete historical here and now, in my concrete encounters.[45]

It goes without saying that this existential self-understanding need not be raised to the level of consciousness. In a hidden way it rules and guides all my caring and willing, all my joy and anxiety, and in every encounter it is called into question. The child who understands itself as a child and understands its begetters as its parents is already sustained by such a self-understanding—in its love, its trust, its feeling of security, its gratitude, its respect, and its obedience. When it is disobedient it gives up this self-understanding, and yet without being able to do so completely, because its self-understanding then makes itself felt in a bad conscience.

This example suffices to show that in existential self-understanding the self understands itself at the same time as it understands what encounters it, whether other persons or the world. As a historically existing self, I am not isolated either from my world or from my own past and future, which in a certain way belong to my world. If it "happens," for example, that in encountering the love of another person, I am given a new self-understanding, "consciousness" is by no means the only thing that "happens"—at least if this is understood as Thielicke and others clearly understand it, as a psychical and not as an existential phenomenon. On the contrary, my whole situation is changed. In understanding myself in this encounter I understand the other person, and so the whole world appears in a "new light," that is, it has in fact become another world. I acquire new insight into my past and my future and a new judgment about them; they are my past and my future in a new sense. I place new demands on myself, and I have a new capacity to be open for encounters. It is clear that I cannot possess such a self-understanding as a timeless truth, for its validity depends on whether it is actualized anew in each particular situation and on whether I understand the imperative meaning that it always contains. *Mutatis mutandis*, one can say: "If we live by the Spirit, let us also walk by the Spirit" (Gal. 5:25).

For the very same thing holds true of the self-understanding of faith, in which we understand ourselves anew through the word that encounters us. And just as in human relations the new self-understanding that is given to me through encounter with another in love and trust remains genuine only when it retains its constant reference to the other person who encounters me, so believing self-understanding never becomes a possession but remains genuine only by constantly responding to the word of God that constantly encounters me and that so proclaims God's act in Christ that it is constantly present.[46] "The goodness of God is new every morning." Indeed it is, but I know about it in a genuine sense only when I acknowledge it anew every morning, for as a timeless truth this statement makes no sense. But this means that I can know about it only as one who is also new every morning—who allows him- or herself to be renewed by it.[47]

The future act of God—so it is objected—also is eliminated by a demythologizing interpretation of New Testament eschatology. I should think on the contrary that the meaning of God's act is thereby first disclosed—at least for those of us who no longer think mythologically. This is so because a demythologizing interpretation makes clear the character of faith as free openness for the future.

Existentialist analysis may well be able to say that free openness for the future is a characteristic of human being insofar as we exist in our authenticity. But is it able by virtue of saying this to give us such openness as concretely existing human beings? It is as little able to do so as it can give us existence at all; it can only say to us that if we want to exist genuinely we must be freely open for the future. It can also remind us of just how frightening this is when it tells us that, for it as philosophical analysis, the future can be defined, finally, as nothing, as our own individual nothing, and when it therefore understands free openness for the future as simply the readiness for anxiety that we each have to take upon ourselves by resolve.

In point of fact, faith is this readiness for anxiety, because faith knows that God encounters us nowhere else than precisely where from our human point of view there is nothing. It is in this sense that Luther interprets the words "we boast of our sufferings" (Rom. 5:3): "Because, then, in many places the Lord is given the name of 'Savior,' helper in suffering, anyone who is unwilling to suffer as much as possible deprives him of his proper titles and names. Thus he will not be Jesus, i.e., Savior, for anyone who does not want to be damned; and he will not be God the Creator for anyone who does not want to be the nothing out of which he may create."[48] In keeping with this Luther holds that "it is the nature of God first to destroy and to annihilate whatever is in us before he gives us of his own."[49] "Those who regard themselves as holy" are persons who "love God with a concupiscent love, i.e., for the sake of their salvation and eternal rest and in order to avoid hell, and thus not for God's sake but for their own." Standing over against such persons are those "who truly love God with a filial love and friendship. . . . such persons submit freely to God's will in all things, even to hell and eternal death, if God should will it, so that his will may be fully done."[50] God "cannot show his power in the elect unless he first shows them their weakness by hiding their power and reducing it to nothing, so that they may not glory in any power of their own."[51] "God saves none but sinners, instructs none but the foolish and stupid, enriches none but paupers, gives life to none but the dead."[52] Of course, the "filial love and friendship" of which Luther speaks does not arise by the resolve whereby we take the readiness for anxiety upon ourselves; it "is not by nature but solely by the Holy Spirit."[53] Thus, readiness for anxiety is given to faith, which is nothing other than freedom from our self (as the old self) for our self (as the new self); as such it is freedom from the illusion that is the ground of sin, that we are able by our own resolve to justify our existence, and therewith is free openness for the future, in keeping with Paul's statement, "Death is swallowed up in victory" (1 Cor. 15:54).

But still the protests do not cease. If God's act can be talked about only as what God does to me here and now, does this not deny that in Christ God has acted once and for all for the whole world? Does this not eliminate the ἐφάπαξ of Rom. 6:10?[54] Is it really the case that I "eliminate the reality of time as a fact once in the past [sic!] from the understanding of the salvation occurrence in the sense of the New Testament"?[55]

It should be clear from what has already been said that I am not talking merely about an idea of God, but am at pains to talk about the living God in whose hands our time is held and who encounters each of us in our time. But insofar as anything more is to be said, it can be put in the single statement that God encounters us in the word, namely, in a specific word, in the proclamation established with Jesus Christ. Of course, it can be said that God encounters us always and everywhere, but we do not see God everywhere unless—as Luther often says—God's word is added and enables us to understand the particular moment in its light. Just as the idea of God's omnipotence and omniscience is not to be realized existentially without the word of God spoken and heard in each and every moment, so this word is not what it is without the moment in which it is spoken. It is not a timeless truth but a specific word that addresses us here and now; its eternity is not its endless duration but its actual presence in every moment. It is God's word only as the word that is happening here and now and not because of its content of ideas—not because, say, it talks about God's grace and kindness (however rightly) but only because it confronts me here and now as judgment or grace. Only in this way is it really the "external word" (verbum externum), for it can be this external word not as a possession that we secure for ourselves by knowledge but only as the address that encounters us again and again.

Just for this reason it is a word spoken to me realiter here and now—whether in the church's proclamation, or in the Bible insofar as it is mediated to me by the church as the word of God addressing me, or through what is said by my Christian brothers and sisters.[56] But this is already to say that this living word of God is not a word of human wisdom but a word that encounters us in history, that its origin is a historical event through which speaking it here and now is authorized and legitimated. This event is Jesus Christ.

That God has acted in Jesus Christ is, however, not a historical fact that can be established objectively. It is not for the objectifying view of the historian that Jesus of Nazareth is the Logos of God.[57] On the contrary, the very fact that in the New Testament the person and work of Christ are described in a mythological conceptuality shows that they cannot be understood in the context of world history if they are to be understood as a divine act of salvation. In fact, the paradox of claiming that they are such an act is that a human figure, even Jesus of Nazareth, and his destiny, which are events in world history and, therefore, can also be perceived by the objectifying view of the historian and can be understood in a world-historical context (see especially John 6:42), nevertheless are not thereby perceived and understood for what they are as God's act, namely, as the eschatological occurrence.

It is as just this occurrence that Jesus Christ is understood in the New Testament (see, for example, Gal. 4:4; John 3:17–19). The only question is whether this understanding is necessarily bound to the representations of cosmological eschatology in which it is formulated in the New Testament writings—with the exception of the Fourth Gospel, for which cosmological eschatology has already become a picture and in which the eschatological occurrence is seen in Jesus' coming as the word, the word of God that becomes present here and now in the proclaimed word. But this demythologizing had already been prepared in the early community by its understanding of itself as the already present people of God of the last days, and thus as the community of the holy. It was carried further by Paul, for whom believers are "a new creation" because the old has passed away and the new has come (2 Cor. 5:17). Henceforth, faith means to exist eschatologically, freed from the world, and to have passed from death to life (1 Cor. 7:29–31; John 5:24; 1 John 4:14). But eschatological existence is realized only by faith, not by sight (2 Cor. 5:7); that is, it is not a worldly phenomenon but is real only in the new self-understanding that comes with faith. As faith in the crucified and risen Christ, this self-understanding is not an independent movement of the human will but is an answer to the word of God that proclaims God's manifest grace in Christ. As the word of God Christ is *ante me et extra me*, although not as a fact that can be objectively stated and chronologically dated *ante me*, but as Christ *pro me*, who encounters me as the word. Thus, the eschatological occurrence that Christ is is always realized only *in concreto,* here and now, where the word is proclaimed (2 Cor. 6:2; John 5:24), whether in faith or in unfaith (2 Cor. 2:15–16; John 3:18; 9:39).

Only in this way is the ἐφάπαξ understood in its true sense as the once of the eschatological occurrence. For it does not mean the datable once of a historical event, but it teaches us—in a highly paradoxical way—to believe in such a once as the once and for all of the eschatological occurrence. As the eschatological ἐφάπαξ this occurrence is constantly present in the proclaiming word. This word says to me—as an event of personal address—that God's prevenient grace has already acted for me, although not in such a way that I can look back on God's act as a datable event of the past but only in the sense that this having acted is now present as an eschatological act.

The word of God is God's word only in the event, and the paradox lies in the fact that it is this word as one and the same word that began with the apostolic preaching and is fixed in scripture and that continues to be borne by human beings in the proclamation, the word of Christ whose content of ideas can also be formulated in general statements.[58] That it is not the first without being the second is the point of the ἐφάπαξ, and that the second is the word of God only when it is the first, only when it becomes event here and now as *viva vox,* is the eschatological point of the ἐφάπαξ.

The word of God and the church belong together, insofar as the church is constituted by the word as the community of the called, and also insofar as proclamation of the word is not the statement of a general truth but rather a proclamation, which as authorized has need of legitimated bearers (2 Cor. 5:18–19). As the word is God's word only as event, so also is the church really the church only as event. It is the eschatological community of the holy and is only paradoxically identical with any sociological phenomenon or institutional structure of world history.[59]

If the task of demythologizing was originally called for by the conflict between the mythological world picture of the Bible and the world picture formed by scientific thinking, it soon became evident that demythologizing is a demand of faith itself. For faith insists on being freed from bondage to every world picture projected by objectifying thinking, whether it is the thinking of myth or the thinking of science. The conflict between these two modes of thinking indicates that faith still has not found its appropriate form of expression, that it has not become conscious that it cannot be proved, that it is not clear about the identity of its ground with its object, that it has not clearly grasped the hiddenness and transcendence of divine action, and that, missing the point of its own "nevertheless," it seeks God's act within the sphere of what is worldly. By criticizing the mythological world picture of the Bible and of the church's traditional proclamation, the modern world picture performs the great service for faith of calling it back to radical reflection on its own essence. It is precisely this call that demythologizing seeks to heed.

The invisibility of God excludes any myth that would make God and God's act visible; as the invisibility *of God*, however, it also excludes any concept of invisibility and mystery that belongs to the conceptuality of objectifying thinking. God eludes the objectifying view and can be believed in only against appearances—just as the justification of the sinner can be believed in only against the accusing conscience.

In point of fact, radical demythologizing is the parallel to the Pauline-Lutheran doctrine of justification through faith alone without the works of the law. Or, rather, it is the consistent application of this doctrine to the field of knowledge. Like the doctrine of justification, it destroys every false security and every false demand for security, whether it is grounded on our good action or on our certain knowledge. Those who would believe in God as their God need to know that they have nothing in hand on the basis of which they could believe, that they are poised, so to speak, in midair and cannot ask for any proof of the truth of the word that addresses them. For the ground and the object of faith are identical. They alone find security who let all security go, who—to speak with Luther—are ready to enter into inner darkness. Just as faith in God as faith in justification rejects separating off certain holy acts, so the same faith as faith in creation rejects separating off certain holy domains among the objects and occurrences of the world. We have learned well through Luther that there are no holy places in the world and that the world as a whole is a profane place—without prejudice to the claim that "the earth everywhere is the Lord's," which can likewise be believed only against appearances. It is not the ordination of the priest that makes the house of God holy but solely the proclaimed word. But in the same way the continuum of nature and history is also profane, and it is only *sub specie* the proclaimed word and against appearances that what has happened or happens in nature or history acquires for believers the character of an act of God or a wonder. Precisely for faith the world becomes profane and is restored to its own lawful regularity as the field for human work. But for just this reason the relation of believers to the world and to the world picture of science is the paradoxical relation of "as if not" (ὡς μή).

NOTES

1. In *Offenbarung und Heilsgeschehen* (1941); reprinted in H. W. Bartsch, ed., *Kerygma und Mythos*, 1 (1948; 2d ed., 1951), 15–48 [in this volume, pp. 1–43]. Naturally, some of the comments are not worth going into. Of those known to me that (with one exception) have appeared since the first edition of *Kerygma und Mythos*, 1, I take the following to be important or characteristic: W. G. Kümmel, "Mythische Rede und Heilsgeschehen im Neuen Testament," *Coniectanea Neotestamentica* 11 (1947); reprinted in H. W. Bartsch, ed., *Kerygma und Mythos*, 2 (1952), 153–69; and "Mythos im Neuen Testament," *Theologische Zeitschrift* 6 (1950): 321–37; K. G. Steck, "Leugnung der Auferstehung?" *Die Stimme der Kirche* (1949): 8: 7–9; 9: 11–12; H. H. Walz, "Das hermeneutische Problem," *Für Arbeit und Besinnung* 3 (1949): 502–17; K. Herbert, *Zur Frage der Entmythologisierung* (1950); H. Diem, *Grundfragen der Hermeneutik* (1950); C. Hartlich and W. Sachs, "Einführung in das Problem der Entmythologisierung," *Für Arbeit und Besinnung* 4 (1950): 353–57, 410–14, 433–36, 480–85, 498–502, 552–57; 5 (1951): 331–48; 6 (1952):50–64; partially reprinted in Bartsch, ed., *Kerygma und Mythos*, 2 (1952), 113–49; W. Wiesner, "Anthropologische oder theologische Schriftauslegung?" *Evangelische Theologie* 10 (1950–51): 49–66; E. Schweizer, "Zur Interpretation des Kreuzes bei R. Bultmann," in *Aux sources de la tradition chrétienne*, Festschrift for M. Goguel (1950), 228–38; A. N. Wilder, "Mythology and New Testament," *Journal of Biblical Literature* 69 (1950): 113–27; K. Grobel, "Bultmann's Problem of New Testament 'Mythology'," *Journal of Biblical Literature* 70 (1951): 99–103; G. Bornkamm and W. Klaas, *Mythos und Evangelium* (1951); E. Steinbach, *Mythos und Geschichte* (1951); F. K. Schumann, "Verkündigung und Auslegung," *Deutsches Pfarrerblatt* (1951): 121–25; and *Wort und Wirklichkeit* (1951); G. Casalis, "Le problème du mythe," *Revue d'histoire et de philosophie religieuse* 31 (1951): 300–342. The best things written on the matter, in my opinion, are the essays of Hartlich and Sachs. I will not go into the essay of E. Stauffer, "Entmythologisierung oder Realtheologie?" *Deutsches Pfarrerblatt* (1949): 413–18; reprinted in Bartsch, ed., *Kerygma und Mythos*, 2 (1952): 13–28; see also the several articles in succeeding issues of the same journal by E.

Gross, L. Thimme, H. W. Bartsch, G. Malfeld, F. Scheidweiler, and R. Fischer: (1949): 486, 513, 541–42, 571–72, 572 (1950): 120; Bartsch's article is reprinted in Bartsch, ed., *Kerygma und Mythos*, 2 (1952), 29–35. I think I could amicably part with Stauffer if only we could each make a confession: I, that I understand nothing about *"Realtheologie,"* and he, that he understands nothing about demythologizing.

2. I may mention that I have tried to advance the discussion somewhat myself in the essays, "Das Problem der Hermeneutik," *Zeitschrift für Theologie und Kirche* 47 (1950): 47–69 [in this volume, pp. 69–93] and "Das Problem des Verhältnisses von Theologie und Verkündigung im Neuen Testament," in *Aux sources de la tradition chrétienne*, Festschrift for M. Goguel (1950), 32–42. As for examples of "existentialist" interpretation, I may also refer to my essays, "Weissagung und Erfüllung," *Studia Theologica* 2 (1949): 1–24; also in *Zeitschrift für Theologie und Kirche* 47 (1950): 360–83; and "Das christologische Bekenntnis des Oekumenischen Rates," *Schweizerische theologische Umschau* (1951): 25–36; also in *Evangelische Theologie* 11 (1951–52): 1–13.

3. See W. Nestle, *Vom Mythos zum Logos* (1940; 2d ed., 1941); also my review in *Theologische Literaturzeitung* 67 (1942): 14–15, and B. Snell in *Gnomon* (1943): 65–76.

4. It is naturally pointless to say that even science's understanding of the world is a "myth." One may call it an "ideology," a "fiction," or something else if one prefers to do so. But the crucial thing is to be clear about the difference in principle between mythical and scientific thinking. Also, one ought not to orient oneself to "the myth of the twentieth century" in order to understand the concept "myth."

5. The comments of Hartlich and Sachs (*Für Arbeit und Besinnung* 5 [1951]: 346) are very good: "In the same way, 'modern scientific thinking' is not identified by the contents of its judgments about nature and the world, but rather by the fact that no judgment about such things may claim to be valid that does not satisfy the demands of sufficient justification. One misses the real point of difference between 'mythological' and 'modern' thinking if one compares the contents of different world pictures and points out that in certain respects the 'modern world picture' is 'not unified,' or 'not closed,' or is even in process of being completely transformed. This is not the point. The insurmountable difference between mythical and modern thinking lies in the diversity of unconscious-uncritical judgments and conscious-critical judgments, even if, for example, the results to which modern natural science may come (significantly, on the basis of conscious-critical judgments) may change within a few years. The world pictures that displace one another in modern science arise as hypotheses on the basis of the critical responsibility of thinking." See also Bartsch, ed., *Kerygma und Mythos*, 2 (1952), 122–23.

6. In keeping with this, the science of history does not reckon with the intervention of God or of the devil or demons. Even if it speaks today, say, of demonic forces, this is only a pictorial way of speaking. It understands the

course of history to be a whole that is closed within itself. Naturally, a nonmaterialistic science of history distinguishes the course of history from the run of nature because it perceives persons and spiritual forces to be the bearers of history. But even if nothing happens in history by physical necessity and the persons who act in it are responsible for their acts, nothing happens without intelligible motivation. Otherwise, even responsibility would be annulled.

7. What has been said may be summarized as Hartlich and Sachs put it (*Für Arbeit und Besinnung* 4 [1950]: 436): "That is 'mythological' which cannot have happened, because it: (1) cannot be established in accordance with the general rules of science (Miracles are impossible.); (2) is contrary to the conditions of the unity of personal life (God's only medium is the spirit in the sense of 'the understandable.' That which is unspiritual cannot be a transmitter of the divine.); (3) is opposed to moral axioms (To think of God as having an inferior morality is to demonize God.); (4) is without any saving meaning relevant to the personal life of the individual (Existentially irrelevant events do not save.)."

8. I cannot concede that my use of the concept "myth" is equivocal (F. K. Schumann, *Deutsches Pfarrerblatt* [1951]: 122). I in no way abandon the sense of "myth" with which I begin in describing myth as a form of thought when I ask for the existentialist point of myth. I could in the same way ask for the existentialist meaning of scientific thinking when I clarify its methodology.

9. There have occasionally been protests against my calling the three-story world picture "mythical." It is certainly correct that a three-story world picture in itself need not be mythical. Yet it actually is so insofar as it is encountered in the realm of mythical thinking. For the upper and lower stories are thought of as "numinous" spheres, and thus as the domains of a transcendent—divine or demonic—reality. Hence it is not at all possible to distinguish between "myth" and "world picture" in the way in which E. Brunner (*Die christliche Lehre von der Schöpfung und Erlösung* [1950], 312) and W. G. Kümmel (*Theologische Zeitschrift* 6 [1950]: 324–25) would like to do. On the other hand, my view does not at all imply that one "would have to call 'mythological' every statement by all the writers of antiquity who lived in the ancient world picture like the authors of the New Testament" (Kümmel, in Bartsch, ed., *Kerygma und Mythos*, 2 [1952], 155). This would not be necessary even if their world picture actually went back to a mythical one; for (at least in the case of Greek antiquity, of which Kümmel is presumably thinking) it had long since been demythologized by becoming a scientific cosmology.

10. Naturally, nothing turns on the term "existentialist"; anyone who is able or willing to do so may find a better term. It should be clear only that what is meant by "existentialist interpretation" is a method of interpreting, a way of asking questions by which interpretation is guided; and there ought not to be a continual confusion of "existentialist" interpretation with an "existential" interpretation. That the conceptuality for an existentialist inter-

pretation is rooted in an existential self-understanding is a problem that remains to be discussed. One may call such interpretation "anthropological" on the condition that what one understands by "anthropology" is existentialist analysis of human being and does not (like W. Wiesner, *Evangelische Theologie* 10 [1950–51]: 49–66) confuse such an analysis with the kind of anthropology offered by objectifying thinking, which can understand human being only as a phenomenon within the world.

11. At the moment I cannot identify the exact wording of this quotation and perhaps owe it to what Herrmann said orally. For the substance of the statement, however, see Wilhelm Herrmann, *Die Wirklichkeit Gottes* (1914), 42: "We cannot make any picture of him [sc. God as omnipotent]. For what an omnipotent being is in itself remains hidden from us. But he has appeared to us in what he has done to us. We can say of God only what he does to us." See also p. 9: "God's reality lies beyond all that science can prove. If we realize this, our faith is not thereby weakened but rather reminded of what is hidden, which is its strength."

12. W. G. Kümmel, in Bartsch, ed., *Kerygma und Mythos*, 2 (1952), 160ff.; also *Theologische Zeitschrift* 6 (1950): 333ff.; H. Thielicke, in Bartsch, ed., *Kerygma und Mythos*, 1 (2d ed., 1951), 188; A. N. Wilder, *Journal of Biblical Literature* 69 (1950): 124.

13. See, for example, J. Schniewind, F. K. Schumann, H. Thielicke, all in Bartsch, ed., *Kerygma und Mythos*, 1 (2d ed., 1951), 79–80, 200, 175ff. According to Thielicke, myth is a form of our thinking that we can never get rid of and that also describes its object in a valid form completely on a par with scientific knowing. This is correct insofar as the thinking of an objectifying science does not grasp the object intended in myth, but it is not correct insofar as it asserts that myth is a form of thinking that adequately expresses its intention. It is precisely the mythical form of thinking that we get rid of by existentialist interpretation. When Schniewind supposes, following Heim and Spengler, that natural scientific representations are also mythological, clearly the difference in principle between mythical and scientific thinking is obscured (see above, pp. 95–97). And when he supposes that concepts like "all" and "source" are mythological concepts because they apply representations of spatio-temporal reality to the transcendent so that they are only "symbols" in religious language, the pertinent question is whether such concepts really do have their source in observation of spatio-temporal reality or rather in the existential thinking of religion.

14. F. K. Schumann (in Bartsch, ed., *Kerygma und Mythos*, 1 [2d ed., 1951], 200) thinks that because the language of proclamation could never be the language of a scientific conceptuality the New Testament reaches "for a language that one may call 'mythological' and that always best expresses what is really involved." It is a "higher order of language," "comparable, say, to that of lyric poetry," "highly indirect, suggestive, and fleeting in comparison with the massive language of objects, again and again sublating itself, as

it were, utterly and completely dependent on our capacity to grasp the unexpressed." But is it only in mythical language that the unexpressed can be uttered? Is it true that demythologizing would not expose but only destroy the point of a statement such as that about the angels who always behold the face of the Father in heaven (Matt. 18:10)?

15. See G. Krüger, *Einsicht und Leidenschaft, Das Wesen des platonischen Denkens* (1939), 55–56, 256–57, 300, and elsewhere. See especially P. Friedländer, *Platon*, 1 (1928), 199–241.

16. In *Kerygma und Mythos*, 1 (2d ed., 1951), 187.

17. Ibid., 85–86.

18. Ibid., 118.

19. Ibid., 179. Examples of naive and unmethodical demythologizing are given by Hartlich and Sachs, *Für Arbeit und Besinnung* 4 (1950): 356, 414, 433–34, 435–36. Reinhold Niebuhr also represents the view (albeit in a thoroughly reflective way) that myth has a symbolic meaning in *Faith and History* (1949). Two examples of his demythologizing interpretation are given on p. 33: "The idea of the divine creation of the world, ... when taken profoundly, describes the limits of the world's rationality and the inadequacy of any 'natural' cause as a sufficient explanation for the irrational givenness of things." The idea of the fall "symbolizes an inevitable and yet not a natural corruption of human freedom."

20. See my essay referred to above in n. 2, "Das Problem der Hermeneutik" [in this volume, pp. 69–93].

21. See above, p. 96.

22. It lies on the same level when there is talk about the mystery of the trinity, which is incomprehensible to human thought and understanding, such as one can occasionally hear in a sermon on Trinity Sunday. Here, too, the concept of mystery is understood in the sense of objectifying thinking. The trinity thus becomes a mere *x* about which neither the preacher nor the hearer is able to think anything; they simply reproduce or accept an unintelligible dogmatic formula from the tradition. But the mystery of God is no *x*, neither one to be figured out nor a definitive one.

23. Existentialist analysis itself knows and demonstrates precisely this.

24. See my essay, "Das Problem der Hermeneutik," referred to above in n. 2 [in this volume, pp.69–93]. I have not been convinced by Hermann Diem (in *Grundfragen der Hermeneutik* [1950]) that the question about the hermeneutical principle is unwarranted; and it especially seems to me to be an evasion when he supposes (p. 20) that the controversy has not been very fruitful about whether there can be a special theological hermeneutics alongside of general hermeneutics. This controversy has to be fought out for the sake of clarity.

25. Here Diem's view is exactly right.

26. In the course of the nineteenth century, interest in hermeneutics more and more receded, and lectures on the subject disappeared from lecture

schedules. To the extent that there was any interest in it, it had to do with specific hermeneutical rules and not with the question about the conceptuality of interpretation and its source.

27. The objections raised by W. Wiesner (*Evangelische Theologie* 10 [1950–51]: 55ff.) all go back to his misunderstanding the point of an existentialist analysis of human existence.

28. Bartsch, ed., *Kerygma und Mythos*, 1 (2d ed., 1951), 197–98.

29. Ibid.

30. Ibid.

31. On the concept of "analogy," see Erich Frank, *Philosophical Understanding and Religious Truth* (1945), 44, 161–64, 179, and elsewhere.

32. See above, p. 98.

33. See *Glauben und Verstehen*, 1 (1933), 214–28, especially 224–25; also W. Herrmann, *Offenbarung und Wunder* (1908), 33ff. Herrmann rightly says that the idea of nature is dissolved by faith in prayer even as by faith in wonders.

34. I could also say "by human subjectivity," assuming that "subjectivity" is to be understood in Søren Kierkegaard's sense as our being as subjects or persons.

35. Neither Wilhelm Herrmann nor Adolf Schlatter meant a merely psychical phenomenon when they talked about "experience."

36. I do not understand Eduard Schweizer (*Aux sources de la tradition chrétienne* [1950], 231) when he speaks of the love awakened by another person as an "innerpsychical process." Love is real only in encounter or in a mutual relationship. Schweizer radically misses the existential meaning of love when he writes: "Love awakens more in a person than an example does; it awakens longing for community, a natural tendency of the I toward the thou, sexuality, or whatever [!]. But in any case it remains an innerpsychical process for which the love of the other person is only the awakening motive. It is true, of course, that in this case not only the intellect, as in the case of teaching, or the imagination, as in the case of an example, but also the affective life is aroused to a much greater extent."

37. See ibid., 235.

38. For example, see n. 11 above.

39. This is not to say, naturally, that the idea of God could not be appropriately grasped outside of faith. It is the explication of the question about God by which human existence is moved. See above, p. 106 and my essay, "Die Frage der natürlichen Offenbarung," in *Offenbarung und Heilsgeschehen* (1941), 1–26.

40. See Diem's protest against a view that supposes it "has the word of God in the Bible even *ante et extra usum*" (*Grundfragen der Hermeneutik* [1950], 5).

41. See above, p. 99.

42. J. Ficker, ed., *Luthers Vorlesung über den Römerbrief 1515/1516, Die Scholien* (1908), 67 (on Rom. 3:5).

43. For example, H. Thielicke, in *Deutsches Pfarrerblatt* (1942): 129ff.;

Bartsch, ed., *Kerygma und Mythos*, 1 (2d ed., 1951), 165–66. Small wonder, then, that the declaration of the Consistory of the Evangelical Confessing Community in Württemberg takes up the same accusation! It is only comic that this declaration thereby refuses from the outset to accept any clarification of a possible misunderstanding.

44. So Thielicke, in the essay just referred to in n. 43. See also my reply to him in *Deutsches Pfarrerblatt* (1943): 3ff.

45. See above, p. 107.

46. Therefore, it is a total misunderstanding when Wiesner supposes (*Evangelische Theologie* 10 [1950–51]: 56, 60) that I reduce the biblical understanding of human existence to a "human self-understanding," that I "secularize" the Christian proclamation, and that I reduce the saving act of God in Christ to the "immanence of human existence and its temporal realization."

47. Eduard Schweizer thinks that I must distinguish in thought "between an act of faith that sees the revelation of the love of God in the occurrence of the cross and a second act of faith for which we are freed by the first and . . . which consists in a radical change in self-understanding" (*Aux sources de la tradition chrétienne* [1950], 236). No, not at any price! For I cannot imagine a believing seeing of the revelation of God's love that would not as such free us for a new self-understanding. How it is to come about that I recognize freedom from sin as valid for me before I "change my self-understanding" (which is what Schweizer actually says, instead of saying "my self-understanding is changed") I find completely unintelligible, and I fear that one must reply here: "You have not yet considered what a heavy weight sin is." The love of God is not a phenomenon in perceiving which we remain the same as we were before. Therefore, the perceiving itself must already be characterized as the work of the Holy Spirit. No proclamation that has "the character of a simple biblical report of what has occurred" can "tell us that this freedom is already a reality prior to and beyond all our understanding" (pp. 237–38). For the reality of that freedom is not something that a report of an occurrence can exhibit. I hope to show presently that Schweizer misunderstands the eschatological meaning of the salvation occurrence.

48. J. Ficker, ed., *Luthers Vorlesung über den Römerbrief 1515/1516, Die Scholien* (1908), 135 (on Rom. 5:4).

49. Ibid., 203 (on Rom. 8:26).

50. Ibid., 217 (on Rom. 9:3).

51. Ibid., 229 (on Rom. 9:17).

52. Ibid., 252 (on Rom. 10:19). See also pp. 206, 216, 245, according to which we human beings are indebted to God as well as to God's creatures, and anyone who would pay this debt "readily and willingly walks into nothingness and death and damnation." See also the quotations from Luther in F. Gogarten, *Die Verkündigung Jesu Christi* (1948), 306–7, 331.

53. Ibid., 217 (on Rom. 9:3).

54. E. Brunner, *Die christliche Lehre von der Schöpfung und Erlösung* (1950);

E. Schweizer, in *Aux sources de la tradition chrétienne* (1950), 231ff.; J. Schniewind, in Bartsch, ed., *Kerygma und Mythos*, 1 (2d ed., 1951), 103ff.

55. W. G. Kümmel, in Bartsch, ed., *Kerygma und Mythos*, 2 (1952), 158, and
in *Theologische Zeitschrift* 6 (1950); also A. N. Wilder, *Journal of Biblical
Literature* 69 (1950): 126–27.

56. It goes without saying that this does not mean that such a word must
always be spoken to me in the same moment of time in which it becomes
decisive for me. Something can become decisive for me now that I heard
yesterday or perhaps even thirty years ago; in that event, it now begins (or
now begins again) to speak to me by proving itself to be a word spoken to my
now.

57. Therefore, I cannot share the interest of Wilder (*Journal of Biblical
Literature* 69 [1950]: 216–17) in the historian's guaranteeing the story of Jesus
historically, anymore than I can share Wiesner's interest (*Evangelische Theologie* 10 [1950–51]: 64–65) in being at least relatively sure about it. When
Wiesner supposes that I turn everything around by my statement, "It is not
because it is the cross of Christ that it is the salvation event; it is because it is
the salvation event that it is the cross of Christ," he is obviously not clear that
the statement about the cross of Christ cannot be a statement of fact but only
a confession.

58. Thus, a human being like myself speaks God's word to me; the logos of
God incarnates itself in him or her. For even the incarnation, as the eschatological event, is not a datable event of the past but an ever new event in the
event of proclamation. I may here refer to my essay, "Das christologische
Bekenntnis des Oekumenischen Rates" (*Evangelische Theologie* 11 [1951–52]:
1–13). In my opinion, christology should at last be liberated in a radical way
from the domination of an ontology of objectifying thinking and set forth in a
new ontological conceptuality.

59. It seems to me that Wilder misses the paradox of this identity when he
charges that the "individualistic character" of my interpretation overlooks the
fact that God's act continually has "a social and corporate reference" (*Eschatology and Ethics in the Teaching of Jesus* [2d ed., 1950], 65). Certainly, God's
act has such a reference, but one must ask in what sense "social and corporate" can be attributed to an eschatological community.

SCIENCE AND EXISTENCE

(1955)

I

By "science" we designate the methodical study of phenomena of the world that encompasses and encounters us—of nature, of history, of humanity, and of the human mind—with the aim of obtaining knowledge of these fields, of knowing the "truth," and thus of knowing how the phenomena "really" are, how they are "in truth," how they are in themselves. By "existence," on the other hand, we designate not merely being available, the fact that something "exists" = is available, but the specifically human way of being, the kind of being belonging to a person whose being is given over to him or her, to whom it can become problematic, who can talk about its being fulfilled or not fulfilled—in short, the responsible, personal kind of being which, as temporal being, also has its own history.

Because science seeks to know phenomena, it makes them the objects of thinking, it "objectifies" them. Scientific thinking thereby disengages itself from immediate encounter with the phenomena and assumes a certain distance over against them—as subject to objects. Thus, for example, the scientist who is an archeologist or a historian of art asks about the material used in a torso of Apollo or about its style in order to locate its place in history, while the poet hears it immediately say to him: "You must change your life" (Rainer Maria Rilke). Nevertheless, scientific thinking is simply the consistent and methodical development of what happens everyday in thinking and talking about the phenomena that encounter us. In objectifying these phenomena we attain our own being as human persons insofar as we understand ourselves to be different from what encounters us. We give names to the phenomena that encounter us and press in upon us and thus stand over against them as subjects—just as the myth of paradise vividly describes our doing when it has Adam give names "to all cattle, and to the birds of the air, and to every beast of the field." Significantly, not one among the other creatures is a fit helper for Adam; he stands over against every one he names as the subject who names and objectifies it, as the human being who is different from it (Gen. 2:20). The objectifying point of giving names is evident everywhere in the history of religion. By giving names to the uncanny powers that press in upon them, primitive men and women objectify the powers, make them disposable for their thinking and accessible to their acting, and so free themselves from anxiety. The demon who has been named can be banished; the God who has been named can be invoked and worshiped.

Objectifying thinking is consistently and methodically developed in science. Because the phenomenon is made an object, the effect that it makes on me or the significance it has for me is excluded. It is the object as it is in itself that is to be seen, and nothing is to be said about me as the subject. In the scientific relation to the object, my reception of it becomes purely passive, that is, a purely receptive, disinterested *seeing* in contradistinction to the *hearing* that attends to what the object may have to say to me about my own personal life. The whole activity of scientific research consists precisely in realizing such disinterested seeing—where "disinterested" means such as to exclude my personal interests. Naturally, I can very well reflect even on the effect and significance of a phenomenon. But then the object of my thinking is precisely the relation of the object to the subject, and precisely this relation is seen in an objectifying way, from a distance.

Now today—not indeed for the first time, but with a special urgency—the question is asked, Is the way of objectifying thinking really the way that leads to knowledge of the essence of phenomena? Does not objectification have its limits, in fact, is it possible at all? Is there any knowledge of phenomena as they are in themselves?

This question has been especially pressed in modern natural science in the area of atomic research. I do not need to go into details here which can be fully understood, finally, only by the specialist. But even a lay person can understand the essential point, namely, that any experiment directed toward establishing the position and the motion of an electron itself influences the electron's motion; the ray of light striking the electron to be observed alters its state of motion. It suffices to become clear—in the words of an expert—that "the more precise the result that an experiment is supposed to yield, the stronger the disturbance it introduces into the phenomenon; the less the phenomenon is supposed to be disturbed, the more it is withdrawn from experimental study. The researcher can never exhaustively experience how the phenomenon is constituted objectively apart from his or her intervention."[1]

II

As in the case of natural science, so also in the case of the science of history the question is raised about the possibility of objective knowledge. In fact, it seems more naturally to arise here, and it is evident to the lay person that real objectivity in historical knowledge cannot be attained. But the question is not quite so simple as it may at first glance appear.

There can be no doubt that in a certain sense the subjectivity of the person studying history colors his or her historical picture. Official historiography during the period of National Socialism had to draw a picture of history that was not only new relative to earlier views but also contradicted them. How, for example, historians of Germany assess the meaning of events and the importance of historical persons, how they distribute predicates expressing value and disvalue, blessing and curse, naturally depends on the ideal picture of Germany and its future that they have in mind and that guides all their evaluations. A Nazi historian projects a different picture than a socialist historian, a conservative a different one than a liberal, an idealist a different one than a materialist, a Protestant a different one than an Ultramontane. Thus, "confused by the hate and favor of parties," the picture of characters such as Martin Luther, Frederick the Great, Napoleon Bonaparte, and Otto von Bismarck continually fluctuates in the writing of history.

To the extent that such pictures of history are expressly tendentious and partisan, like those of National Socialism or of Bolshevism, they fall outside of our discussion about the possibility of objective historical knowledge. They make a principle out of the fact that no one can be completely free from subjective prejudices, even though any science of history striving for objectivity is at pains to exclude such prejudices as far as they can be excluded. That and in what sense even such a science cannot attain an objectivity that is free from subjectivity now has to be clarified.

To begin with one could ask, Is there really no objective knowledge of historical truth? Are not the processes and actions of history well established by all kinds of historical documents? Cannot scientific research, then, objectively know the real course of historical events? Can it not know, as Leopold von Ranke wanted to do, how it really was? In point of fact, strictly methodical research can objectively know a certain side of historical process, namely, to the extent that historical phenomena are nothing more than events that have taken place in space and time and that can be spatially and temporally fixed. That and when Socrates drank the cup of hemlock, that and when Caesar crossed the Rubicon, that and when this or that battle took place or this or that catastrophe occurred can all be objectively established. Nor may one object that many events cannot be exactly described and fixed and that only relative certainty can be attained, either because the sources are inadequate or ambiguous or because the historian's discernment and gift for putting things together naturally have their limits. For none of this means anything in principle. In this sphere, methodical historical research can in principle attain objective knowledge.

But is what is properly called "history" adequately seen when the only thing in view is the field of events that can be fixed in space and time—when, in other words, the writing of history is simply chronicle or narration? It is not, first of all, because history is in any case also a movement or process in which individual processes do not simply stand alongside one another or follow one another without any connection but are connected as cause and effect, and because such connection between them presupposes the effective working of certain forces. Such forces as are effective in the movements of history are also easy to perceive. The first great historian of the West, Thucydides, already knew how human drives and passions are the moving forces of history. Everywhere social exigencies, economic needs, and individual as well as group ambition and struggle for power are factors that determine the historical process, along with ideas and ideals. In assessing such factors the views of historians differ, and a court that could decide which of them is right does not exist.

But then, second, it belongs to a historical event that it has a meaning in the continuous course of history, a meaning that first raises it to the rank of a historical event. What did it mean for the history of Athens, indeed, for the history of the human spirit, that Socrates drank the cup of hemlock? What did it mean for the history of Rome, indeed for the history of the West, that Caesar crossed the Rubicon in 49 B.C.? Does not a judgment about this depend on the subjective standpoint of the historian? Must we say, then, that objective historical knowledge is not to be attained?

III

I would not say that historical phenomena are ambiguous, but they are many-sided. They can be seen under several aspects, under different perspectives. And this is so because human beings themselves are complex. They consist of body and soul (or if one prefers, of body, soul, and spirit); they are possessed of drives and reason; they have material and spiritual needs, wishes, and imagination. They are political and social beings, and they are at the same time individuals, each with his or her own uniqueness, so that the community between them can be seen not only as political and social but also as personal. It is just as possible, therefore, to see and describe history as political history as to see and describe it as the history of economics, the history of problems, the history of ideas, or the history of individuals and personalities. Psychological as well as ethical standards, biographical and also aesthetic interests can all be effective in historical presentations. Each of these ways of looking at history is open to one side of the phenomena, and something objectively right becomes evident under every aspect (provided there are not any methodical errors). The picture is falsified only when one way of looking is absolutized and turned into a dogma.

The course of historiography is such that, after overcoming a purely chronological and narrative presentation, the political point of view comes to dominate, because the movement of history first comes to consciousness in connection with political changes. Other points of view can then become dominant as reactions, whereupon emerge the history of ideas, the history of economics, and so on. Finally, modern history attempts to unite various points of view, under the heading, say, of general history of culture. Such a unity is in principle conceivable. Of course, if it is not to be a merely external combination of points of view, which stand alongside or alternate with one another, it presupposes a basic view of the essence of history such as we today still have not achieved. In practice, a certain way of asking questions will always guide each individual historian, and there is nothing to object to in this, provided this way is not absolutized and the historian remains conscious that he or she sees the object from a certain perspective, alongside of which other perspectives, also, are not only justified but necessary.

In every perspective something objectively right is seen. The subjectivity of historians (given the strictness of their methods) does not mean that they see falsely, but only that they choose certain perspectives and proceed by certain ways of asking questions. Without such, however, no picture of history can be projected at all, insofar as it seeks to get beyond a merely chronological and narrative presentation and tries to show the play of forces in the course of events and their connection. To this extent one can say that in the science of history, also, analogously to physics, the subject participates in the accomplishment of knowledge. Historians do not photograph history anymore than painters photograph a face or a landscape that they seek to paint.

IV

Beyond this moment of perspective, however, there is still something else to think about that I like to call the moment of "existential encounter." In projecting a scientific picture of history, historians participate with their own existence, for historical phenomena are not what they are as such—precisely as historical phenomena—without the historical subjects who understand them.

It is not enough to say that phenomena become historical because they are seen in a certain perspective and understood as parts of a continuum of events. This view is in danger of missing the real essence of historical occurrences and understanding the course of history by analogy with the course of nature, as was (or is) the case in so-called historicism. Even in the choice of a perspective, what we call the "existence" of historians will usually play a role, and we must now try to make clear what is meant by their existence in the sense of their existential encounter with history.

History speaks in the sense of disclosing its essence only to those who themselves stand in history and participate in it. Only to them are historical phenomena visible in their meaning. This does not mean, naturally, that the subjects who understand the phenomena ascribe a meaning to them by subjective preference that they do not have in themselves. On the contrary, it needs to become clear that the genuine relation of historians to history cannot be understood according to the traditional scheme of the relation of subject to object.

Events or figures of the past are not historical phenomena at all simply "in themselves," not even as parts of a causal continuum. They are historical phenomena only in their relatedness to the future, for which they have meaning and for which the present has responsibility. One can say, then, that to every historical phenomenon belongs its own future in which it first shows itself for what it is; more exactly, in which it *more and more* shows itself for what it is. For it will definitively show itself for what it is only when history has reached its end.

It is understandable, therefore, that the question about the meaning of the course of history and of the events that go to form it first received an answer, in fact, was first really asked as a question, on the basis of a view that thought it knew the end of history, namely, Jewish–Christian eschatology. Pagan antiquity still had not asked this question, and it is well known that its philosophical thinking had not yet developed any philosophy of history. Such a development first occurred in the domain of Christianity, just because it thought it knew the end of history. In modern times this eschatological way of looking at history has been secularized by Georg Wilhelm Friedrich Hegel as well as by Karl Marx, both of whom in their ways supposed they knew the end of history and on this basis interpreted the course of historical events.[2]

If we today no longer presume to know the goal and end of history and, therefore, regard the question about the meaning of history as a whole as meaningless, still the question about the meaning of our own history, as the history out of which we come, is not only meaningful but imperative. It is the question about the meaning of the historical phenomena on which we look back for the present, which is called to responsibility by the future. Such a question can be answered only by each new present, but it also demands to be answered. And with this insight we can at last answer the question, Why should there be any science of history, anyhow?

Possible examples are: the breakdown of a unified medieval culture in view of our problem of the relation of the confessions and of education; or the breakdown of the medieval world view in view of our question of how we today are to understand ourselves in relation to the world; or the French Revolution in view of our question about the authoritarian ordering of the state; or the rise of capitalism and socialism in view of our problem of ordering the economy.

By means of this kind of historical reflection, the phenomena of the past become real historical phenomena and begin to disclose their meaning. But this means that objectivity in historical knowledge is not to be attained either in the sense of conclusive knowledge or even in the sense that a phenomenon in its being in itself is perceived by the historian in some purely receptive way. There simply is not any such being in itself of a real historical phenomenon.

It will be clear that this does not mean that historical knowledge is subjective in the sense that it depends on the individual preference of the historian who is its "subject." If the historical way of asking questions grows out of the historical life of the responsible historian, it includes a readiness to hear the claim that is encountered in the historical phenomenon. For just this reason the demand applying to all scientific research, that it be conducted without presuppositions, also applies to historical research. Of course, historians may not presuppose the results of their work but must silence any of their own personal wishes with respect to its results. But this does not mean that they have to quench their personal individuality for the sake of the objectivity of their knowledge. On the contrary, genuine historical understanding presupposes the utmost liveliness of the "subjects" who understand, the richest possible unfolding of their individuality. Only those are able to understand history who are themselves moved by sharing in history, that is, who are open to the language of history by their own responsibilities for the future. In this sense it is precisely the "most subjective" interpretation of history that is the "most objective." Those alone who are moved by the question of their own historical existence are able to attend to history's claim.

Even in this case understanding history gives rise to a scientific, "objectifying" presentation. For even in this case the knowledge acquired is not a product of the "subjects," not a projection into the past of their own fantasies, but emerges out of their encounter with history, whose claim they hear. The living participation of historians in history, their existential encounter with it, shifts into the role of a means for acquiring "objective" historical knowledge. Thus historians who are involved the most intensively and the most passionately force themselves to a perceiving that attains the highest degree of objectivity. It is only so that they can submit their knowledge to others to be accepted or criticized, instead of carrying on a monologue or falling into lyrical declamations. All scientific research is subject to discussion, by which all acquired knowledge has to be confirmed.

V

But is there also a kind of thinking and talking that is in principle not objectifying? There is, indeed, insofar as there is a perceiving that does not take place in the distance of disinterestedness, in the passivity of mere receptiveness, but in which the interested activity of the person, of existence, is controlling. But is this not also the case with the genuine understanding of history that we have just been considering? Certainly. But while such understanding soon becomes the means to an objectifying presentation and submits its knowledge to discussion, there is an existential understanding that is solely my own and out of which there can indeed arise a practical way of leading my life but not any objectifying presentation.

Consider a simple example. That my father is my father can apparently be objectively established and also perceived through observation. But that he is *my* father can finally be perceived only by a single person, namely, by *me*, not through disinterested observation but only in the personal encounter in which he is father to me and I allow him to be my father. Or, to take another example, were I to want to make certain of the friendship of a friend through observation, through psychological analysis, say, I would have already destroyed the relation of friendship, which can be grounded only in mutual trust. From the standpoint of objectifying seeing, such trust includes a risk. But without such a risk there cannot be any personal relation at all between one person and another. A young man who sought to learn about his (future) bride through the information provided by a detective bureau would learn nothing at all about her personal being, because it does not disclose itself to objectifying seeing but only to existential encounter.

A watch that my father once gave me is, for objectifying seeing, a watch like others, or what is distinctive about it can be determined by means of a classification of watches and according to certain objective standards, such as being of Swiss manufacture, having a works constructed in such and such a way, and being worth so and so much money. It can be exchanged for any other watch similarly constructed and of similar worth, and it can be replaced by such a watch if I happen to lose it. But as the gift made to me by my father, it is neither exchangeable nor replaceable; for precisely what it is for me as my father's gift cannot be exchanged or replaced. In it I continually encounter my father's love and kindness, which are experienceable as such only in the encounter.

Were I to say that it can still be objectively established that the watch is the gift of my father, this certainly would not be false. But by including my father's love and kindness within the domain of objectifying thinking, I nullify their proper character, which they have only as encountering me. This can be seen easily enough where a son, who establishes his father's kindness as an objective fact and on that basis presumes to do all sorts of things, such as running up debts, because he reckons with his father's kindness, does not perceive it at all. For if he did, his father's being father to him would not be a license for his imprudence and arbitrariness but would be a judgment condemning him, as it is for the prodigal son in Jesus' parable, in which true and false sonship are set over against one another. The true way of being a son precisely does not reckon with the father's being father; for the true son it is not an objective datum that could ground any "on the basis of which."

If I have my authentic being, my existence, in being personal—and this means also in personal relations—it can be said that my existence is not objectifiable. Naturally, one can very well reflect on existence objectively, in that one reflects on what it means in general or on the essence of existence. But such reflection knows that existence itself is always my own and can be taken over or actualized only by me, and this means that existence is an ever new event in the decisions of the moment. It is nothing merely available but something that happens ever anew. My being as father or as son, as spouse or as friend does not flow along as a natural process but is constantly in question and can be won or lost only by my own decisions. The continuity proper to it is not natural but historical, although this does not mean, naturally, that the decisions always have to be conscious.

Decision consists in grasping the situation, or the moment, in which my existence as a self or person is demanded of me. This already makes clear that the nonobjectifiability of existential decision does not mean its utter subjectivity, that it is not a complete arbitrariness to which no "objective" reality corresponds.[3] The reality here, however, is not the reality that can be perceived by objectifying seeing but the reality of encounter. No historical or sociological analysis of the situation can answer my question about what is demanded of me here and now, although such an analysis can also be demanded so that I become aware of the possibilities for my concrete decision. But insofar as what is demanded of me is not *something*—such as my vote for some party in an election or a decision to assume a certain office—but (in all of these) is *myself*, no analysis can take away from me the responsibility for my decision. Just the reverse can be true, namely, that when I know it is myself that is demanded of me and do not close myself against the demand, I can for the first time see calmly and clearly the possibilities and conditions of practical decision.

Just as this holds good both for decisions within the narrowest circle of personal encounters and for the spheres of social and political life in which I have to exist as a person, so it also holds good for encounter with destiny. How I accept my destiny and endure it, opening myself to it or closing myself against it, is always a matter of decision here and now. If one wants to say that it is a matter of world view or of faith, the fact remains that maintaining one's world view or faith is itself always a matter of decision. For no one possesses a world view or faith in the way in which one possesses scientific knowledge. They are again and again called into question by one's concrete encounters with destiny, and they are genuine only in that they again and again become an event.

The decision demanded of me in the moment in a certain way tears me out of the continuum of my course of life. I say "in a certain way," because the decision also always involves assuming an attitude toward my previous existence, to which I have to remain faithful or from which I am supposed to turn away to a new life. But because the continuum of my existence is called into question by a new encounter—not in its "that" but in its "how"—the moment of decision is an isolated, or, better, a new now; and my decision cannot be derived simply from what has gone before in the way in which scientific knowledge can be the result of knowledge already given.

This fact indicates still another difference between existential perceiving and objectifying thinking. The latter understands its object in the context of the domain of objects to which it belongs. Thus, for objectifying thinking a phenomenon is not understood and is a mere x or enigma until it can be located in some definite place in the order proper to some domain of objects. Nothing can be new here in a radical sense; each individual thing is to some extent already foreseen in the outline that always guides the study of objects in a particular domain. A phenomenon can be new only in the sense that it appears as a new constellation of the possibilities or effective forces that are given in this particular field. But the possibilities are limited. If something appears that cannot be made understandable on the basis of the possibilities previously known (or assumed), objectifying science cannot be content simply to accept this fact or to assume the encroachment of some transcendent power. The upshot, rather, is what is called a "crisis in the foundations" of the particular science. This means that the science in question revises its presuppositions; it recognizes that the guiding outline by which its field of objects was previously circumscribed is no longer adequate, and it develops a new outline in which the phenomenon that proved enigmatic in the old one now becomes understandable.

Phenomena stand still, so to speak, for objectifying seeing. I say "so to speak," because I can naturally subject a process of motion to objectifying seeing, in which case the whole process of motion is what is made to stand still. This is clear in an experiment through which processes of motion are produced at will for the purpose of observation. They have to put up, so to speak, with being objects to be observed.

But existential events do not stand still and do not put up with being produced as objects for observation. Hence, the risk involved in a personal relation of trust and love. I cannot first look at the trust that encounters me or the love that is given me in order on that basis to establish that the person encountering me is trustworthy and kind; rather, I can know the trust extended to me or the love given to me only in the openness of trusting in return.

I also cannot look at my own decisions but can only make them. To those who suppose that they can avoid the risk of decision by establishing objectively what they have to do and have already done, Luther says, "Sin bravely!" (*Pecca fortiter*). If prior to our decision we reflect on ourselves as deciders, we have thereby already made a decision, although this does not mean, naturally, that we do not each have to ask ourselves, Can I take responsibility for this or for that? In questioning myself in this way, however, I have already made a decision to accept responsibility. I also cannot look back on my decisions by objectifying seeing and write a testimonial to whether I have or have not decided rightly. Rather, I must constantly assume the risk, whether my decision was right or wrong (see 1 Cor. 4:4). The appropriate look back cannot be taken by objectifying reflection but can only force itself upon me by my conscience which accuses me.

VI

I hope it has become clear that there can be a thinking and talking about existence only in the sense that the concept of existence is made explicit—as I have, in fact, attempted to explicate it by the foregoing comments. It is evident from them that existence by its very meaning is my own existence, which I can never talk *about* but can always only talk *out of*.

This implies for theology the insight that talk about God is not possible as objectifying talk. Naturally, even as in reference to existence, I can very well develop the meaning of the idea of God and of faith in God. But I cannot talk in an objectifying way about God, who only encounters me in the word of God that affects me in my existence. I can talk of God only out of my existence, in fear and trembling, in trust and gratitude. I cannot establish God's kindness objectively so that I can reckon with it. It is not any "on the basis of which" for my conduct. I can recognize it as kindness only in the decision of faith, in the surrender of myself. I cannot know God's omnipotence by objectifying perception and reckon with it, as in the statement one often hears, "If God is omnipotent, then he can do even this or that." Rather, I can acknowledge God's omnipotence only as one who has been overwhelmed by God in my own existence.

God is not a reality that has a place within the cosmic continuum so that God could be thought of as necessary to this continuum, even if as the head thereof. God does not stand still and does not put up with being made an object of observation. One cannot *see* God; one can only *hear* God. God's invisibility is not due to the inadequacy of our organs of perception but is God's being removed in principle from the domain of objectifying thinking. God's revelation is revelation only *in actu* and is never a matter of God's having already been revealed. Those who believe God's word have *certitudo* in the existential act of faith, but they have no *securitas*. For God is not to be held fast in faith in the sense that believers can look back on their faith as a decision made once and for all. God always remains beyond what has once been grasped, which means that the decision of faith is genuine only as actualized ever anew. God is "the guest who always moves on" (Rilke), who cannot be apprehended in any now as one who remains. Rather, as the one who demands my decision ever anew, God ever stands before me as one who is coming, and this constant futurity of God is God's transcendence.

NOTES

1. H. Kneser, *Theologische Rundschau*, N.F. 8 (1936): 308.
2. See K. Löwith, *Meaning in History* (1949).
3. Such a misunderstanding may perhaps be present in J. P. Sartre, but I do not wish to judge this.

IS EXEGESIS WITHOUT
PRESUPPOSITIONS
POSSIBLE?

(1957)

The question whether exegesis without presuppositions is possible must be answered affirmatively if "without presuppositions" means "without presupposing the results of exegesis." In this sense, exegesis without presuppositions is not only possible but imperative. In another sense, however, no exegesis is without presuppositions, because the exegete is not a *tabula rasa* but approaches the text with specific questions or with a specific way of asking questions and thus has a certain idea of the subject matter with which the text is concerned.[1]

I

1. The demand that exegesis must be without presuppositions in the sense that it must not presuppose its results (we can also say that it must be without prejudices) needs only brief clarification. This demand means, first of all, the rejection of allegorical interpretation.[2] If Philo finds the Stoic idea of the apathetic sage in the prescription of the law that the sacrificial animal must be unblemished (*Spec. Leg.* 1:260), it is clear that he does not hear what the text says but lets it say only what he already knows. And the same is true of Paul's exegesis of Deut. 25:4 as a prescription that preachers of the gospel are to be supported by congregations (1 Cor. 9:9) or of the interpretation in the Letter of Barnabas (9:7–8) of the 318 servants of Abraham (Gen. 14:14) as a prophecy of the cross of Christ.

2. But even where allegorical interpretation is given up, exegesis is

frequently guided by prejudices.[3] This is so, for example, when it is presupposed that the evangelists Matthew and John were personal disciples of Jesus and that the stories and sayings of Jesus that they transmit must be historically true reports. In this case, it must be affirmed, for instance, that the cleansing of the Temple, which in Matthew is placed during Jesus' last days just before his passion, but in John stands at the beginning of his ministry, took place twice. The question of an unprejudiced exegesis becomes especially urgent when the problem of Jesus' messianic consciousness is concerned. May exegesis of the Gospels be guided by the dogmatic presupposition that Jesus was the Messiah and was conscious of being so? Or must it rather leave this question open? The answer should be clear. Any such messianic consciousness would be a historical fact and could be shown to be such only by historical research. Were research to make it probable that Jesus knew himself to be the Messiah, this result would have only relative certainty, for historical research can never endow it with absolute validity. All historical knowledge is subject to discussion; consequently, the question whether Jesus knew himself to be the Messiah remains an open question for exegesis. No exegesis that is guided by dogmatic prejudices hears what the text says but lets it say only what the exegete wants to hear.

II

1. The question of exegesis without presuppositions in the sense of unprejudiced exegesis must be distinguished from this same question in the other sense in which it can be asked. And in this other sense we must say that there cannot be any such thing as exegesis without presuppositions. That there is no such exegesis in fact, because every exegete is determined by his or her own individuality in the sense of special biases and habits, gifts and weaknesses, has no significance in principle. Individuality in this sense is the very thing the exegete ought to eliminate by self-education, by learning to listen with the kind of hearing that is interested in nothing except the subject matter of the text. But invariably presupposed in this is the historical method of questioning the text. Indeed, exegesis as the interpretation of historical texts is a part of the science of history.

Of course, it belongs to historical method that a text is interpreted in accordance with the rules of grammar and of the use of words. And closely connected with this is the demand that historical exegesis also inquire about the individual style of a text. The sayings of Jesus in the Synoptic Gospels, for example, have a different style from the Johannine ones. This is connected with another problem that exegesis has to take into account. Paying attention to the use of words, to grammar, and to style soon leads to the observation that every text speaks in the language of its time and of its historical setting. This the exegete must know; therefore, he or she must know the historical conditions of the language of the period out of which a text has arisen. This means that for an understanding of the language of the New Testament the acute question is, Where and to what extent is its Greek determined by a Semitic use of language? Out of this question grows the demand to study apocalypticism, rabbinic literature, and the Qumran texts as well as the history of Hellenistic religion.

Examples are hardly necessary, and I cite only one. The New Testament word $\pi\nu\epsilon\hat{\nu}\mu\alpha$ is rendered in German as *Geist*. This explains why the exegesis of the nineteenth century (for example, in the Tübingen school) interpreted the New Testament on the basis of the idealism that goes back to ancient Greece, until Hermann Gunkel pointed out in 1888 that $\pi\nu\epsilon\hat{\nu}\mu\alpha$ in the New Testament meant something utterly different—namely, God's wonderful power and manner of acting.[4]

Historical method includes the presupposition that history is a unity in the sense of a closed continuum in which individual events are connected by the succession of cause and effect. This does not mean that the process of history is determined by causal law and that there are no free human decisions that determine the course of events. But even a free decision does not happen without a cause or motive; and the task of the historian is to come to know the motives of human actions. All decisions and acts have their causes and consequences; historical method presupposes that it is possible in principle to exhibit them and their connection and thus to understand the whole historical process as a closed unity.

This closedness means that the continuum of historical happenings cannot be broken by the interference of supernatural powers from beyond the world and that, therefore, there is no "wonder" in this sense of the word. Such a wonder would be an event whose cause did not lie within history. While, for example, the Old Testament narrative talks about God's intervention in history, the science of history cannot assert such an act of God but perceives only that there are those who believe in God and in God's action. To be sure, as the science of history it may not assert that such faith is an illusion and that there is no act of God in history. But as science it cannot itself perceive such an act and proceed as though such had occurred; it can only leave everyone free to decide whether he or she wants to see an act of God in a historical event that it itself understands in terms of the event's immanent historical causes.

It is in accordance with such a method that the science of history goes to work on all historical documents. There can be no exceptions in the case of biblical texts if they are to be understood at all historically. Nor can one object that the biblical writings do not intend to be historical documents but rather are witnesses of faith and proclamation. Of course they are. But if they are ever to be understood as such, they must first be interpreted historically, because they speak in a strange language, in concepts of a faraway time, of a world picture that is alien to us. Simply put, they must be *translated*, and translation is the work of the science of history.

2. If we speak of translation, however, we are faced at once with the hermeneutical problem.[5] To translate means to make understandable, and this presupposes an understanding. The understanding of history as a continuum of causes and effects presupposes an understanding of the effective forces that connect individual phenomena. Such forces are economic needs, social exigencies, the striving for political power, human passions, ideas, and ideals. Historians differ in assessing such factors, and in any effort to achieve a unified view the individual historian is guided by some particular way of asking questions, some particular perspective.

This does not mean a falsification of the historical picture, provided that the perspective that is presupposed is not a prejudice but a way of asking questions, and that the historian is aware that this way of asking questions is one-sided in questioning the phenomenon or the text from this one particular perspective. The historical picture is falsified only when a particular way of asking questions is taken to be the only one—when, for example, all history is reduced to economic history. Historical phenomena are many-sided. Events like the Reformation can be observed from the viewpoint of church history as well as of political history, of economic history as well as of the history of philosophy. Mysticism can be studied from the viewpoint of its significance for the history of art, and so on. But if history is to be understood at all, some particular way of asking questions is always presupposed.

Furthermore, the forces that are effective in connecting phenomena are understandable only if the phenomena themselves, which are connected thereby, are also understood. This means that an understanding of the subject matter itself belongs to historical understanding. Can one understand political history without having concepts of the state and of justice, which by their very nature are not historical products but ideas? Can one understand economic history without having a concept of what economy and society in general mean? Can one understand the history of religion or of philosophy without knowing what religion or philosophy is? One cannot understand Martin Luther's posting of the Ninety-Five Theses in 1517, for instance, without understanding what it meant to protest against the Catholicism of his time. One cannot understand the Communist Manifesto of 1848 without understanding the principles of capitalism and socialism. One cannot understand the decisions of persons who act in history if one does not understand human beings and their possibilities. In short, historical understanding presupposes an understanding of the subject matter of history itself and of the men and women who act in history.

This is to say, however, that historical understanding always presupposes that the interpreter has a relation to the subject matter that is (directly or indirectly) expressed in the text. This relation is grounded in the life context in which the interpreter stands. Only someone who lives in a state or in a society can understand the political and social phenomena of the past and their history, just as only someone who has a relation to music can understand a text having to do with music, and so on.

Therefore, a particular understanding of the subject matter of the text, grounded in a life relation to it, is always presupposed by exegesis; and to this extent no exegesis is without presuppositions. I call this understanding a "preunderstanding." It no more involves prejudice than does the choice of a particular perspective. The historical picture would be falsified only if the exegete were to take his or her preunderstanding to be a definitive understanding. The life relation is genuine, however, only when it is alive, which is to say, only when the subject matter with which the text is concerned is of concern to us and is a problem for us. If we question history out of a lively concern with our own problems, it really begins to speak to us. Through discussion with the past it comes alive, and in learning to know history we learn to know our own present: historical knowledge is at the same time knowledge of ourselves. To understand history is possible only for one who does not stand over against it as a neutral, nonparticipating spectator but also stands within it and shares responsibility for it. We speak of this encounter with history that grows out of one's own historicity as the "existential encounter." The historian participates in it with the whole of his or her existence.

This existential relation to history is the basic presupposition for understanding it.[6] This does not mean that understanding history is "subjective" in the sense that it depends on the personal preference of the historian and thereby loses all objective significance. On the contrary, it means that history can be understood precisely in its objective content only by a subject who is existentially concerned and alive. It means that the scheme of subject and object that has validity for natural science is not valid for historical understanding.[7]

What has been said includes an important insight, namely, that historical knowledge is never closed or definitive anymore than is the preunderstanding with which the historian approaches historical phenomena in asking about them. If historical phenomena are not facts that can be neutrally observed but rather disclose themselves in their meaning only to one who approaches them alive with questions, they are always understandable only now in that they speak anew to every present situation. Indeed, the questioning itself arises out of the historical situation, out of the claim of the now, out of the problem that is given in the now. For this reason historical research is never closed but must always be carried further. Naturally, there are certain items of historical knowledge that can be taken as definitively known, namely, such items as concern only events that can be fixed chronologically and locally, as, for example, the assassination of Julius Caesar or Luther's posting of the Ninety-Five Theses. But what these events *mean* as historical events cannot be definitively fixed.

Hence, one must say that a historical event can be known for what it is—precisely as a historical event—only in the future. And one may also say that the future of a historical event belongs to it.

Naturally, items of historical knowledge can be transmitted, not as definitively known but in such a way as to clarify and expand the succeeding generation's preunderstanding. Even so they are subject to criticism by the following generation. Can we today foresee the meaning of the two world wars? No. For what a historical event means always becomes clear only in the future. It can show itself definitively only when history has come to an end.

III

What are the consequences of this analysis for the exegesis of biblical writings? They may be formulated in the following theses:

1. The exegesis of biblical writings, like any other interpretation of a text, must be unprejudiced.

2. However, the exegesis is not without presuppositions, because as historical interpretation it presupposes the method of historical-critical research.

3. Further presupposed is the exegete's life relation to the subject matter with which the Bible is concerned and therewith a preunderstanding.

4. This preunderstanding is not closed but open, so that there can be an existential encounter with the text and an existential decision.

5. Understanding of the text is never definitive but rather remains open because the meaning of scripture discloses itself anew in every future.

After what has already been said nothing needs to be added to clarify the first and the second of these theses.

As regards the third, the preunderstanding in question is grounded in the question about God that is alive in human life. This does not mean that the exegete has to know everything possible about God but only that he or she is moved by the existential question about God, whatever its conscious form—whether as the question about "salvation" or about deliverance from death, or about certainty in the face of an ever-shifting destiny, or about truth in the midst of an enigmatic world.

With regard to the fourth thesis, existential encounter with the text can lead to a "yes" as well as to a "no," to confessing faith as well as to express unfaith, because in the text the exegete encounters a claim, or is offered a self-understanding that can be accepted (as a gift) or rejected, and therefore has to make a decision. Even in the case of a "no," however, the understanding is legitimate, because it is a genuine answer to the question of the text, which, being an existential decision, is not to be refuted by argument.

So far as the fifth thesis is concerned, because the text speaks to existence, it is never definitively understood. The existential decision out of which the interpretation emerges cannot be transmitted but must always be made anew. This does not mean, of course, that there can be no continuity in the exegesis of scripture. It goes without saying that the results of methodical historical-critical research can be transmitted, even if they can be taken over only by constantly being critically tested. But even with respect to exegesis that is grounded existentially, there is also continuity insofar as it provides guidance for posterity—as has been done, for example, by Luther's understanding of the Pauline doctrine of justification through faith alone. Just as this understanding must be reached ever anew in discussion with Catholic exegesis, so every genuine exegesis that offers itself as a guide is at the same time a question that must always be answered anew and independently. Because the exegete exists historically and must hear the word of scripture as spoken to his or her special historical situation, he or she will understand the old word ever anew. Ever anew it will make clear who we are and who God is, and the exegete will have to express this in an ever new conceptuality. Thus, it is true even of scripture that it is what it is only with its history and its future.

NOTES

1. Walter Baumgartner, to whom the following pages are dedicated, has published an essay entitled "Die Auslegung des Alten Testaments im Streit der Gegenwart," *Schweizerische theologische Umschau* 11 (1941): 17–38. Because I quite agree with what he says there I hope he will concur if I attempt to carry the hermeneutical discussion somewhat further.

2. Of course, if there is an allegory in the text, it is to be explained as an

allegory. But such explanation is not allegorical interpretation; it simply asks for the meaning intended by the text.

3. A criticism of such prejudiced exegesis is the chief concern of the essay by Baumgartner referred to above (n. 1).

4. H. Gunkel, *Die Wirkungen des Heiligen Geistes nach der populären Anschauung der apostolischen Zeit und der Lehre des Apostels Paulus* (1888; 3d ed., 1909).

5. Compare with what follows my essays "Das Problem der Hermeneutik" in *Glauben und Verstehen*, 2 (1952): 211–35 [in this volume, pp. 69–93] and "Wissenschaft und Existenz" in *Ehrfurcht vor dem Leben, Festschrift für Albert Schweitzer* (1955), 30–45 [in this volume, pp. 131–44]. Finally, see chapter 8 of my *History and Eschatology* (1957).

6. It goes without saying that the existential relation to history does not have to be raised to the level of consciousness. It may only be spoiled by reflection.

7. I do not go into certain special questions here, such as how an existential relation to history can already be present in the research of grammar, lexicography, statistics, chronology, or geography or how the historian of mathematics or physics participates existentially in the objects of research. One thinks of Plato!

ON THE PROBLEM
OF DEMYTHOLOGIZING

(1961)

I

By "demythologizing" I understand a hermeneutical procedure that inquires about the reality referred to by mythological statements or texts. This presupposes that myth indeed talks about a reality, but in an inadequate way. It also presupposes a specific understanding of reality.

"Reality" can be understood in a double sense. We commonly understand it to mean the reality of the world as represented in objectifying seeing. This is the reality in which we find ourselves as human beings, in which we orient ourselves by standing over against it, and with whose continuum of happenings we reckon in order to control it and thereby to secure our life. This way of looking at reality is fully developed in natural science and in the technology it makes possible.

Simply as such, this way of seeing reality is demythologizing because it excludes the working of supernatural powers—whether it be the working of powers that create and sustain natural processes or the working of powers that disrupt these processes. A thoroughgoing natural science has no need of the "God hypothesis" (Pierre Simon de Laplace) because it understands the forces that govern natural processes to be immanent within them. Likewise, it eliminates the idea of wonder as a miracle that disrupts the causal continuum of the world process.

Like all the other phenomena in the environing world, human existence itself can be subjected to objectifying seeing insofar as it appears within the world. We then stand over against ourselves, making ourselves an object. In this way we reduce our authentic, distinctive reality to the reality of the world. This happens, for example, in an "explaining" psychology (as distinct from an "understanding" psychology in Wilhelm Dilthey's sense) and in sociology.

This way of looking at reality can also become controlling in the science of history, and, in fact, is so in a positivistic historicism. Here the historian stands over against history as a subject observing an object, thereby becoming a spectator outside of the historical process as it follows its course in time.

Today we have more and more come to recognize that there is no such stance, because the act of perceiving a historical process is itself a historical act. The distance required for neutral observation of an object is impossible. The apparently objective picture of historical processes is always conditioned by the individuality of the observer, who also is historical and can never be a spectator who stands outside of historical time.

I cannot go into the question of whether there is an analogous understanding of the subject-object relation in modern natural science that has recognized that what is observed is already formed or modified in some way by the observer. The exact extent of this analogy between modern historical and natural science would require special investigation. The point here is simply that in the modern understanding of history reality is understood in a different way from the way of objectifying seeing, namely, it is understood as the reality of human beings who exist historically.

Distinctively human being is different in principle from the being of nature perceived through objectifying seeing. We are accustomed today to speak of specifically human being as "existence," by which we mean not merely being available in the sense in which plants and animals also "exist" but the mode of being that is distinctively human.

Unlike any such natural being, we human beings do not simply take our place in the causal continuum of natural processes but must ourselves each take over our own being and are responsible for it. This means that human life is history; through ever new decisions it leads into a future in which we each choose ourselves. These decisions are made in accordance with the way in which we each understand our existence or in keeping with what we each see to be the fulfillment of our life.

History is the field of human decisions. It is understood when it is seen as such, when we recognize that at work in it are the possibilities of human self-understanding—possibilities that are also possibilities of self-understanding in the present and that cannot even be perceived except in unity with present self-understanding. I call any such interpretation of history "existentialist interpretation," because, motivated by the existential question of the interpreter, it asks for the understanding of existence that is at work in a given history.

Since all human beings in fact come out of a past in which certain possibilities of self-understanding are already controlling, in that they are offered or called in question, decision is also always a decision with respect to the past—indeed, finally, with respect to each human being's own particular past and future.

To be sure, this decision does not need to be made consciously, and in most cases is unconscious. In fact, it can appear as decisionlessness, which is actually an unconscious decision for the past, a fallenness into bondage to the past. This means, however, that a human being can exist either authentically or inauthentically, and just this possibility of being authentic or inauthentic belongs to historicity as the distinctively human reality.

If authentic human being is an existence in which we each take over ourselves and are responsible for ourselves, authentic existence includes openness for the future or the freedom that becomes event in every new present. Hence, our human reality as historical is never finished like that of an animal, which is always what it is utterly and completely. Rather, our reality is our history; it constantly stands before us so that being future can be said to be the reality in which we stand.

This becomes clear in human history from the fact that the historical meaning of an event can be understood only from the standpoint of its future. Its future belongs to the very essence of the event. Therefore, the meaning of historical processes is to be definitively understood only from the end of history. Since, however, such a view from the end of history is not possible for human seeing, a philosophy that endeavors to understand the meaning of history is likewise impossible. The meaning of history can be talked about only as the meaning of the moment, which is meaningful as the moment of decision.

All decisions, however, are made in concrete situations, and even the decisionless behavior of inauthentic existence always takes place in just such situations. If, then, the science of history seeks to clarify the possibilities of self-understanding that are manifested by human decisions, it must also present the concrete situations of past history. But these situations disclose themselves only to an objectifying view of the past. Even if such a view cannot grasp the historical meaning of an act or an event, it nevertheless can and must seek to know the sheer facts of acts and events and, in *this* sense, to establish "how it really was." Furthermore, even if the continuum of human actions is not determined by causal necessity, it still is connected by the sequence of cause and effect. No event, no act of will, no decision is without a cause. Even a free decision follows from reasons if it is not to be blind caprice. Hence, it is always possible to look back at the course of history and to understand it as a closed causal continuum; in fact, this is the way an objectifying view of history has to look at it.

The question now is whether existentialist interpretation of history and objectifying presentation of history are mutually contradictory. Does the reality seen in the one case so contradict the reality seen in the other that one must speak of two realms of reality or even of a double truth? This would clearly be a wrong inference, for there is in fact only *one* reality and only *one* truth of the statements about the same phenomenon.

The one reality, however, can be seen under a double aspect in accordance with our double possibility as human beings of existing authentically or inauthentically. In inauthentic existence we understand ourselves in terms of the world that stands at our disposal, whereas in authentic existence we understand ourselves in terms of the future of which we cannot dispose. Correspondingly, we can look at the history of the past in an objectifying way or else as personal address, insofar as in it the possibilities of human self-understanding become perceptible and summon us to responsible choice.

The relation of these two modes of self-understanding must be characterized as "dialectical," insofar as the one is never given without the other. The human being whose authentic life is realized in decisions is also a being with a body. Responsible decisions are made only in concrete situations in which our bodily life is also at stake. The decision in which we choose ourselves, our authentic existence, is always simultaneously the decision for a possibility of life in the body. Responsibility for ourselves is always simultaneously responsibility for the world and its history. For the sake of our responsibility we have need of an objectifying view of the world in which we are placed, which is the "work world" that stands at our disposal. But precisely herein lies the temptation of regarding this work world as authentic reality and of missing our authentic existence and attempting to secure our life by disposing of what stands at our disposal.

Therefore, it is quite clear that existentialist interpretation of history has need of objectifying observation of the historical past. Even if such observation cannot grasp the historical meaning of an act or an event, existentialist interpretation is equally unable to dispense with the (most reliable possible) determination of facts. Friedrich Nietzsche's antipositivistic statement that there are no facts but only interpretations is open to misunderstanding. If one means by "fact" a historical fact in the full sense, inclusive of its meaning and its significance in the continuum of historical processes, the statement is correct. In this sense a fact is always an "interpretation," a picture drawn by the historian who is personally involved in it. But an interpretation clearly is not a creature of fantasy but the interpretation of something, and this something to be interpreted is the "fact" that (within whatever limits) is accessible to the historian's objectifying view.

II

If this may be assumed as valid, it is possible to solve the problem of demythologizing also with respect to the science of history. Is the science of history like natural science in demythologizing simply as such? Yes and no.

History as such demythologizes to the extent that it views the historical process in an objectifying way and thus understands it as a closed continuum of causes and effects. The historian cannot proceed otherwise if he or she wants to achieve reliable knowledge of some particular fact—for example, by determining whether some traditional account is really a valid testimony to a certain fact of the past. Thus, the historian cannot allow that the continuum of historical happenings is broken by the interference of supernatural powers nor can he or she acknowledge any wonders in the sense of events whose causes do not lie within history. Unlike the biblical writings, the science of history cannot talk about an act of God that intervenes in the historical process. What it can perceive as a historical phenomenon is not God's act but only faith in God's act. Whether there is any reality corresponding to such faith it cannot know, since any reality that lies beyond the reality visible to an objectifying view is for it invisible. It must regard as mythology all talk about the action of transcendent powers as something that can be observed and established in the world accessible to an objectifying view and also used, say, as an argument in support of certain truths. Likewise mythological for the science of history is any talk of otherworldly spheres, such as heaven and hell, that are spatially tacked on to the visible world.

Even so, there is a difference in principle from the position of natural science in relation to myth: whereas natural science eliminates myth, the science of history has to interpret it. History must raise the question of the point of mythological talk, which, after all, is a historical phenomenon.

This question as to the point of mythological talk may be answered quite simply. Myth intends to talk about a reality which lies beyond the reality that can be objectified, observed, and controlled, and which is of decisive significance for human existence. It is the reality that means for us salvation or damnation, grace or wrath, and that demands of us respect and obedience.

I can disregard here the etiological myths that seek to explain striking natural phenomena or appearances. They are significant in the present context only insofar as they permit us to understand mythological thinking as the kind of thinking that arises out of awe, fright, and questioning and that thinks in terms of the continuum of cause and effect. Such thinking can be characterized as a primitive form of science, just as many students seek to reduce mythology in general to primitive thinking.

This primitive scientific and thus also objectifying thinking is, in fact, peculiar to all mythology. But there is also a difference in principle. It must be asked, namely, whether or to what extent the intention of myth is simply to talk about the world that we observe and control so as in some way to explain it or whether it intends to talk about our own reality as human beings and thus about our own existence. In the present context, myth is under discussion to the extent that it expresses a certain understanding of human existence.

But what understanding of existence? It is an understanding in which we find ourselves in a world filled with enigmas and mysteries and in which we experience a destiny that is equally enigmatic and mysterious. We are forced to recognize that we are not lords of our life, and we become aware that the world and our life have their ground and limit in a transcendent power that lies (or powers that lie) beyond whatever we can reckon with and dispose of.

Mythological thinking, however, naively objectifies what is thus beyond the world as though it were something within the world. Against its real intention it represents the transcendent as distant in space and as only quantitatively superior to human power. By contrast, demythologizing seeks to bring out myth's real intention to talk about our own authentic reality as human beings.

Is there a limit to demythologizing? It is often said that neither religion nor Christian faith can dispense with mythological talk. But why not? Such talk does indeed provide pictures and symbols for religious poetry and for cultic and liturgical language in which pious devotion may sense a certain amount of meaning. But the decisive point is that these pictures and symbols conceal a meaning which it is the task of philosophical and theological reflection to make clear. Furthermore, this meaning cannot be reexpressed only in mythological language, for if it is, the meaning of this language also must be interpreted—and so on *in infinitum*.

The claim that myth is indispensable implies that there are myths that are not subject to existentialist interpretation. And this means that in certain cases, at least, it is necessary to talk about the transcendent, or deity, in objectifying terms, since mythology is an objectifying way of talking.

Can this be correct? Everything turns on the question of whether talking about God's act is of necessity mythological or whether it, too, can and must be subject to existentialist interpretation.

Because God is not a phenomenon within the world that can be objectively established, God's act can be talked about only if we at the same time talk about our own existence as affected by God's act. One may call this way of talking about God's act "analogical." In this way one may express that being affected by God has its origin solely in God and that we ourselves are merely passive recipients.

Even so, it must be maintained that being affected by God's act can be talked about only as an existential event that cannot be established or proved objectively. Of course, every such existential encounter takes place in a concrete situation, and it is easy or, so to say, natural for the person encountered by God to refer this situation also to God's act. This is perfectly legitimate, provided only that originating in God's will is not confused with the causality accessible to an objectifying view. To speak of a "wonder" here—although not of a "miracle"—is entirely justified.

Just as faith talks about wonder, so it also talks and must talk about God's act as Creator and as Lord of nature and history. If we know in our own existence that we ourselves are called into life and upheld by God's omnipotent power, we also know that the nature and history within which our life takes place are governed by God's act. But this knowledge can be expressed only as a confession and never as a general truth, like a theory in natural science or in the philosophy of history. Otherwise God's act would be objectified into a process within the world. The statement that God is Creator and Lord has its legitimate basis only in our existential self-understanding.

So understood, however, the statement contains a "paradox." It asserts the paradoxical identity of an occurrence within the world with the act of the God who stands beyond the world. Indeed, faith asserts that it sees an act of God in an event or in processes that at the same time, for an objectifying view, can be established as processes within the continuum of natural and historical happenings. Thus, for faith, the act of God is a wonder in which the natural continuum of processes in the world is, as it were, sublated.

The peculiar thing about Christian faith, however, is that it sees an utterly special act of God in a certain historical event, which as such can be objectively established. This is the appearance of Jesus Christ, who is seen to be the revelation of God that calls everyone to faith. The paradox of this claim is expressed most sharply in the Johannine statement, "the word became flesh."

Clearly, this paradox is of a different kind from the other one that claims that God's action is everywhere and at all times indirectly identical with the world process. The Christ occurrence means the eschatological occurrence through which God has put an end to the world and its history. Therefore, this paradox is the claim that a historical event is at the same time the eschatological event.

The question now is whether this event can be understood as an event that takes place in one's own unique existence, or whether, for the person called to faith, it remains an object over against a subject in the manner of worldly reality. In the second case it would be an event of the past that is made present, or "remembered," through the objectifying view of the historian. If, on the other hand, it is to be understood as an event that affects me in my own unique existence, it has to be or be able to become present in some other sense.

But just this is involved in its meaning as an eschatological event. As such it cannot be or become an event of the past, provided historical events can never have the meaning of ἐφάπαξ (once and for all), which belongs to the nature of the Christ event as an eschatological event.

Therefore, unlike other historical events, it cannot be made present through "remembrance." Rather, it becomes present in the proclamation (or the kerygma), which has its origin in the event itself and without which the event is not at all what it is. This means that the proclamation itself is eschatological occurrence. In it, as personal address, the event Jesus Christ becomes present ever anew—as an event affecting me in my own unique existence.

The bearer of the proclamation is the church, and here the paradox is repeated. For under one aspect the church is a phenomenon at the disposal of an objectifying view, while in its real nature it is an eschatological phenomenon—or, better, an eschatological event that occurs ever anew in every new moment.

I therefore agree with Enrico Castelli "that the 'kerygma' calls for the being of the event (as much as mystery); and the eventual analysis of the event does not encroach on the revelation because it is the revelation of the message and of the event (that is, of the history) at the same time."

INDEX

Alpirsbach, 62
Apocalypticism, 2, 14, 19, 147
Aristotle, 70, 77
Ast, Friedrich, 80
Auerbach, Erich, 80
Augustine, 87, 106

Barth, Karl, vii, 9, 37, 88–90
Baumgartner, Walter, 152
Blättner, Fritz, 80
Boeckh, August, 80
Burckhardt, Jacob, 77, 80

Castelli, Enrico, 163
Christ occurrence, 21, 30–42 passim, 59. *See also* Demythologizing; Eschatological occurrence; God, God's act; Jesus Christ; Salvation occurrence
Church, 14, 41, 42, 62, 65, 119, 120, 121, 163. *See also* Proclamation
Context of life, 74–75, 89. *See also* Exegesis; Hermeneutics; Interpretation

Death, 6–7, 16
Decision, 6, 15, 23, 106, 108, 110, 112, 141–44, 151, 152, 156–58. *See also* Faith; Human existence; Self-understanding
Demythologizing, 3, 9, 11–12, 15, 99, 101–4, 105, 117–18, 155, 161; already within the New Testament, 11, 19, 33–41, 120–21; as

demanded by faith, 102, 121–23; earlier attempts at, 11–14, 21; as not picking and choosing, 8–9; objections to, 99–119; as posed by conflicting world pictures, 2–8, 121–22; as posed by myth, 9–10, 99, 160–61; as posed by the New Testament, 10–11, 32–33, 102. *See also* Christ occurrence; Existentialist interpretation; Myth, Mythology; Science; Theology; World picture
Dilthey, Wilhelm, 22–23, 69–90 passim, 156
Dinkler, Erich, 45
Dualism, 14–15

Enlightenment, the, 3, 25
Eschatological occurrence, 34, 38–42, 54, 120–21, 163. *See also* Christ occurrence; Jesus Christ; God, God's act; Proclamation; Salvation occurrence
Eschatology, 5, 19, 61, 120, 137
Exegesis, 85, 87, 90, 103, 145–52. *See also* Hermeneutics; Interpretation; History; Understanding
Existentialist analysis, 23, 82, 87–88, 89, 93, 107–9, 116, 117, 118. *See also* Human existence
Existentialist interpretation, 9, 14–15, 21, 88–90, 99–106 passim, 125–26, 157–59, 161. *See also* Demythologizing; Myth, Mythology

Faith: as answer to the proclamation, 40, 57, 102, 114–15, 117, 120; as authentic human nature, 23–26; Christian, 21, 30, 50, 51, 162; as decision, 19, 20, 112, 141-42, 144, 152; of Easter, 39–40; as eschatological existence, 19, 26, 30, 41; as existential encounter, 144; as existential self-understanding, 103–5, 115–17; as faith in justification, 55, 57–58; as *fides qua/quae creditur*, 51–54; as freedom, 17–20, 21, 30–31; justification by faith alone, 122, 152; language of, 100, 103; as a mode of existing, 55–56; New Testament understanding of, 17–21; as trust and obedience, 17–18, 21; and unfaith, 39, 56, 59, 114, 121, 152; as working through love, 20, 24. *See also* Decision; Human existence; Self-understanding
Fallenness, 15, 26, 27–30, 157
Feuerbach, Ludwig, 89
Fourth Gospel, 120. *See also* John
Friedländer, Paul, 80

Gnosticism, 2, 8, 14–16, 18, 19, 28, 38
God, God's act; as eschatological occurrence, 54, 59, 61, 120, 121, 163; as existential encounter, 110–11, 113–14, 119, 162; existential question about, 50–51, 66, 87, 106, 109, 128, 151; as future, 117, 144; as ground and object of faith, 54; as immanent, 42, 111; knowledge of, 50–51, 54, 87, 144; as mystery, 104–5; as not objectifiable, 7, 49–50, 99, 102, 111, 122, 143, 144; as revealed, 50, 53, 144; talk about/of, 32, 99–100, 110–23, 143–44, 162–63; as transcendent, 42, 98, 122, 144. *See also* Christ occurrence; Eschatological occurrence; Jesus Christ; Salvation occurrence
Grimm, Hermann, 81
Gunkel, Hermann, 147

Harnack, Adolf von, 12

Hegel, G. W. F., 107, 137
Heidegger, Martin, 23, 25, 28, 82
Herder, J. G. von, 72, 81
Hermeneutics, 69–70, 71, 73, 79, 83, 85, 86, 103, 148. *See also* Exegesis; Historical method; History; Interpretation; Theology; Understanding
Herrmann, Wilhelm, 3, 54, 89, 99, 114, 115
Historical method, 146–48, 151, 152
Historicism, 78, 81, 137, 156
Historiography, 133, 135
History: as closed continuum of cause and effect, 137; 147–48, 158, 159–60; historian's existential encounter with, 85, 87, 136–42, 150, 151–52; meaning of, 135, 137–38, 157–58; objective knowledge of, 85, 133–35, 138, 139; as open to the future, 137–38, 150–51, 156; science of, 47, 48, 53, 89, 133–38, 146–51, 156–60. *See also* Hermeneutics; Interpretation; Understanding
History-of-Religions School, 13–14, 21
Human existence: as authentic/inauthentic, 8, 17, 23, 24–30, 102, 107, 112, 117, 140–41, 157–59; Christian understanding of, 11, 15–20; as existence in the face of death, 26–27, 28; existential question about, 50, 83, 106, 107, 108; as historical being, 28, 113, 131; as nature/spirit, 5–8; philosophical understanding of, 21–32, 87, 107–10. *See also* Decision; Existentialist analysis; Faith; Self-understanding; Understanding

Idealism, 3, 6–7, 21, 25, 26, 28, 107, 147
Intention of the text, 76–77, 79, 83. *See also* Exegesis; Hermeneutics, Interpretation
Interpretation, 69–93 passim, 145–53 passim; allegorical, 12, 145–46, 152–53; genuine, 79–81, 85; objec-

tive of, 74, 83; as reconstruction, 71, 83; sources for, 76, 79, 88. *See also* Context of Life; Exegesis; Hermeneutics; History; Intention of the text; Life relation; Preunderstanding; Questions, ways of looking/asking; Self-understanding; Theology; Understanding

Jaspers, Karl, 23
Jesus Christ: cross of, 32–36, 130; as cultic symbol, 13–14; death of, 7, 10, 35, 36–38; as eschatological occurrence, 54, 120–21, 163; as event of proclamation, 119–20, 162; as God's decisive act, 12–13, 14, 119–20, 162; messianic consciousness of, 146; as paradox/history and myth, 32–42, 111–12, 162–63; preexistence of, 7, 8, 10, 32–33, 101; resurrection of, 7, 32, 36–41, 89; as salvation occurrence, 33, 139; virgin birth of, 10, 33, 101. *See also* Christ occurrence; Demythologizing; Eschatological occurrence; God, God's act; Salvation occurrence
John, 8, 19, 26, 30, 31, 32, 37, 40, 60. *See also* Fourth Gospel
Jonas, Hans, 15

Kamlah, Wilhelm, 23–28, 32
Kaufmann, Fritz, 82
Kerygma, 11, 12, 14, 46, 60–64, 163. *See also* Proclamation
Kierkegaard, Soren, 23, 25
Klaas, Walter, 99

Language, 70, 100, 101, 103
Laplace, Pierre Simon de, 155
Liberalism, 12, 53
Life relation, 48, 71–76, 82, 86, 88, 104, 106, 149–51. *See also* Exegesis; Interpretation; Preunderstanding; Understanding
Löwith, Karl, 80
Luke, 53
Luther, Martin, 25, 115, 116, 118, 119, 122, 143, 152

Marx, Karl, 137
Matthew, 33
Melanchthon, Philipp, 99
Misch, Georg, 72
Myth, Mythology, 2, 9–10, 14–15, 32, 33, 95–99, 125, 126, 155, 160–61; and cult, 42, 97–99; impossibility of repristinating, 2–8, 11; of the New Testament, 1–5; as objectifying seeing and thinking, 10, 42, 98–99, 100, 101–2, 111; and science, 3–5, 95–98, 99, 101; and symbols, 100, 110–11. *See also* Christ occurrence; Demythologizing; Eschatology; Existentialist interpretation; World picture

National Socialism, 81, 133
Naturalism, 6–8
Niebuhr, Reinhold, 127
Nietzsche, Friedrich, 159

Old Marburgers, viii
Otto, Rudolf, 51, 52

Pantheism, 81, 111–12
Patzer, Harald, 70
Paul, 1–43 passim, 57, 60, 118, 120, 122, 145, 152
Philology, 59, 70–71, 103
Philosophy, 49, 58–59, 78
Plato, 52
Preunderstanding, 72–74, 77, 82–84, 86–87, 148–51. *See also* Exegesis; Interpretation; History; Life relation
Proclamation, 1–42 passim, 54, 58, 87–88, 102, 106, 108, 111–12, 114–15, 120, 121, 163

Questions, ways of looking/asking (perspective/point of view), 33, 72–73, 76–77, 78, 79, 81, 84–85, 135–36, 137, 138, 148–49. *See also* Exegesis, Interpretation

Reformation, the, 148–49
Relativism, 81
Religion, 13–14, 51–52

Romanticism, 3, 81

Sacraments, 6, 7, 8, 35, 38, 97
Salvation occurrence, 2, 8, 13, 14, 21,
    23, 26, 34–36, 39, 100, 115, 119. *See
    also* Christ occurrence; Demythol-
    ogizing; Eschatological occur-
    rence; God, God's act; Jesus Christ
Science, 3, 4, 45–49, 103, 131, 155,
    156; as objectifying seeing and
    thinking, 46–47, 69, 84, 98–99, 101,
    103, 113, 131–33, 156. *See also*
    Hermeneutics; History; Interpre-
    tation; Theology; Understanding
Schlatter, Adolf, 103
Schleiermacher, Friedrich, 51–52,
    69–93 passim
Schniewind, F. K., 108–10
Self-understanding, 39, 47, 57, 60, 63,
    64, 65, 87–88, 104–5, 108, 109,
    115–17, 126, 129, 152, 157, 158–59,
    162. *See also* Faith; Human
    existence; Understanding
Spengler, Oswald, 81
Synoptic Gospels, 147

Theology, ix, 49–67 passim; Chris-
    tian, 50; liberal, 12; New Testa-
ment, 61–64, 65; nineteenth-cen-
    tury, 11–12; object of, 49–54, 66;
    Old Testament, 63–64; paradox of,
    55, 56, 66–67; practical, 65; as
    scientific study of church history,
    64–65; systematic, 59–61, 61–63,
    65; task of, ix, 3, 11, 14, 54, 57, 58,
    59. *See also* Demythologizing;
    Hermeneutics; Interpretation
Thielicke, Helmut, 100–101, 116
Thucydides, 134
Troeltsch, Ernst, 51
Tübingen, 147

Understanding, 69–93 passim; exis-
    tential, 82, 93, 108, 139; historical,
    35, 149–51; participatory, 77–78,
    84; prescientific, 47–48, 50, 67, 104;
    scientific, 70, 84, 113. *See also* Self-
    understanding, Preunderstanding

Wartenburg, Graf Yorck von, 22–23,
    80, 82
Winckelmann, J. J., 72, 80–81
World picture, 1–8, 9, 41, 42, 51, 96,
    99, 101, 102, 121–22, 123, 124, 125
World view, 3, 6, 12, 41, 57, 111–12,
    138, 141